THE PURPLE RAINBOW
A Book About Hurt
A Book About Love

THE PURPLE RAINBOW

A Book About Hurt
A Book About Love

Patrick J. Brennan

THE THOMAS MORE PRESS
Chicago, Illinois

ISBN 0-88347-247-3

TABLE OF CONTENTS

For Dr. Zirpoli
and Jerry
and especially Dawn,
who have given me
a glimpse of
the reason to live
and the reason to die.

PREFACE

I WANT to dedicate this book to the many clients whose composite stories are reflected in the case studies of this book. All of the stories in this book are essentially true; but they are mosaics—mosaic stories, crafted from the pieces of many different stories. None of the depth of pain or the joy of victory is fabricated. I also dedicate this book to Dr. Robert Zirpoli, a great source of comfort and challenge to me over the years. It was he who first introduced me to the notions of insights into self, decision-making, and behavior change. In addition, I dedicate this book to Father Jerry Broccolo, mentor and spiritual director, who was a corrective figure in my life, and who first introduced me to the love of God. And finally, I again dedicate a book to my long-time friend and associate, Dawn Mayer. This dedication is from a different standpoint than other books. Not only do I thank her for typing and editing my manuscript. I write in awe and admiration of her strength of character, sacrificial love, and depth of faith. This book in many ways is about her, though the stories are not hers. She has entered into ''the greatest suffering,'' with great trust that God's grace always washes people ashore. Already glory and beauty are being spoken through her woundedness. For her great prophetic message to me and those who know her, I, we, are eternally grateful.

—Patrick Brennan
February 1989

CHAPTER ONE

Coming Apart: Emotional Divorce
On Becoming Strangers

Joyce sat across from me. A look of shock was on her face. After twenty years of marriage, Frank, her husband, had just told her that he did not know if he wanted to be married anymore. The initial shock was to get much worse as the days, weeks, and months went by. Frank's diffidence about staying married was compounded by the later revelation that someone else had come into his life—another woman with whom he had become intimate. Joyce's hurt, during this time, often turned to rage, as she compared her years of emotional investment in the family and marriage with his now wandering spirit.

Joyce and Frank resemble many couples that I have seen over the years. Actually there was an erosion going on between the two of them for years. Joyce had things "on automatic," doing her marriage and parenting without much change in style over the course of two decades. For Frank, things were changing a lot inside. Yet he was unable to share with his wife the emotional turbulence he was experiencing. In effect, they had become, as so many couples are, "intimate strangers." Though they continued sexual activity with each other, these were not really lovemaking experiences.

Where was the breakdown? How had things gotten so bad? Perhaps the core dysfunctional dynamic was Joyce's assumption that a relationship remains static, unchanging, and Frank's actual changing but inability to share this change or talk about it. For years, they had been "becoming divorced," though they did not even realize it. Studies of divorce have revealed that rather than being a legal entity, divorce is a process of erosion.

Joyce's death experience was obvious. She had been steadfast and faithful in her commitment to Frank. As we have talked over the past months, she has vented a great deal of anger, rage, hurt, and loneliness. There has been very little I can do to remove those painful emotions, except listen. There is a mysterious component to guiding, helping, mentoring, counseling, being with others in pain. Often just the act of listening lances wounds and allows some of the painful emotions to drain out.

Frank had his own pain: the guilt of infidelity, the remorse he felt over hurting his wife and his children. But his was a unique kind of pain. What was exploding in Frank, even though he was and is in midlife, was his first genuine experience of intimacy—in this case, with "the other woman." Most of his life he had played the tough, stereotypical, dominant macho, without much awareness of or sensitivity to his own inner world. Frank and Joyce each were living with a stranger—each other. Each also had a stranger within—perhaps Frank more than Joyce. There were feelings and a shadow/stranger self in Frank that he has had to face.

The Pain of Decision-Making

Awakening to the spousal friend turned stranger and the stranger within are two painful experiences in marriage. In the midst of their pain, both Frank and Joyce are facing the inevitability of another source of struggle: a decision. Each must decide what the future will be—for them as individuals and as a couple. Frank especially is hedging on deciding. A decision for the marriage will exclude the new-found intimacy he has found with the third party. A decision for the newly-found friend is a decision to dissolve the marriage. Joyce, on the other hand, has decided that the marriage is no longer viable. Though she is devastated, she must get on with life for herself and her children. Frank is maximizing his pain with his refusal to make decisions. He is operating out of that unwritten law that so many of us use to procrastinate: maybe things will work out. *Things* never work out! People can make decisions they hope are life-giving and pain-reducing.

Frank and Joyce: each with a stranger within, each living with a stranger, each confronted with the prophetic power, the life-shaping power of making decisions. Relative to the stranger within, one is only fully free when he or she has begun to meet and accept that interior stranger. Many of us are blocked when it comes to communication or intimacy because we are not what Carl

Rogers called "congruent" with ourselves or self-aware. Getting to know the stranger within involves accepting all of one's emotions—realizing that feelings in and of themselves are morally neutral; rather it is what we do with them that may become hurtful and destructive. Accepting the stranger within involves confronting "the shadow" side, and seeing the potential for good and grace even in that part of ourselves which we find difficult to accept or admit to. Facing the stranger within means confronting our subtle sin, and seeking God's help in overcoming or changing that dimension of ourselves. Facing the stranger within involves coming to grips with hurting memories, in effect a hurt or wounded child in us, still in need of healing. In a process sort of way, we need to deliberately attend to that hurting past, and call on God for help and healing.

Making Space and Time

For Frank and Joyce to get to know the stranger that each has become for each other, they both would need to make a radical commitment to give and share something with each other: time. Time—couple time, family time, friendship time—time is of the essence for the growth and development of any relationship. John Paul II in his encyclical on the family, *Familiari Consortio,* the United States' Bishops recent statement on the family, the fine work of Dolores Curran, and other resources warn about other institutions replacing the family, replacing marriage in the performance of nurturing, caring functions. With so many institutions doing for us, we have little time to be with each other. Thus, the stranger syndrome sets in. One of my mid-life students at the Loyola Institute of Pastoral Studies in Chicago said in a class recently that it was a frightening experience for her to realize her adolescent children and her husband had become strangers to her. The absence of time with them had created walls of estrangement and alienation.

Decisions as Prophecy and Art

Let us return to the issue of decision-making for a moment. The power to make decisions is, indeed, a prophetic, artistic dimension to life. We literally shape our lives by the decisions that we make. Making decisions, like every act of prophecy or work of art, necessitates pain and struggle. A real birthing goes on in every decision. Like Frank, many people feel that they can alleviate pain by not making decisions. On the contrary, a refusal to decide holds one in stagnation or paralysis. Not to decide is an attempt to have it all, in Frank's case—to have both marriage and extra-curricular lover. Joyce's attempt to prayerfully and with guidance decide is her attempt to move on. While one can decide poorly or impulsively (and this needs to be avoided), healthy, integral decision-making is life-giving.

The pain of decision-making is that every "yes" to one thing is a "no" to another. For Frank, yes to marriage is "no" to the lover, and vice versa. While decision-making can indeed be life-giving, it is also true that before life can be reached there is the passageway of death. Every decision is paschal in nature, involving life, death, and resurrection. When Joyce chooses divorce, as perhaps the most life-giving direction for her, her attempt at new life is at the same time plunging her into a void or abyss of grief and loss that will be acutely felt before healing begins.

The Toxic Nature of Resentments

Tony and Carol likewise had to make marital decisions. After several sessions with them, I realized that Tony was willing to work out the marriage. He had allowed himself and Carol to become strangers to each other; but he had grown in his desire to invest, to work at it. There is a bitter foe working against the reconciliation of strangers, the finding of quality time, and the making of life-giving decisions. That foe is resentment. Carol communicates that she would rather hold on to the past than move in a positive, life-giving direction. "I'm finished trying," she barked at me, "and don't try to make me try this anymore. Fix him!" She pointed to Tony and said, "Fix him!" We can hold on to the past, or freeze ourselves in an unpleasant, unhealthy status quo by dwelling in resentment or bearing grudges.

A.A. and other twelve-step processes speak of certain defects of character or moral failings that we cannot remove through our own efforts or will power. In a real sense, we need to pray for the ability to forgive or to be released from the demonic hold of resentments on the human spirit. Tony and Carol are going to stay together;

but their union will be an unstable, unsatisfactory one. Tony's efforts to grow and change as an individual and a couple will be met by the seething undercurrent of Carol's resentful anger. Resentment blocks therapeutic decisions and activities.

The Failure Bred by Success

Joe and Kathy are another couple in the throes of emotional divorce. Missing in their relationship is something that we touched on before: time. Joe is successful, but honestly confesses that he does not know whether "he has success or success has him." Advancement in career is usually looked on as an apparent blessing; but quite often it is a subtle curse. Successful people, without restraint, easily fall into the syndrome of becoming strangers to and with the people whom they call family or friends. The rationalization Joe uses with Kathy is that all he does is done so that Kathy and the kids can have the nice things that they have. Kathy tearfully retorted recently that she and the children would settle for fewer things if they could only have more of Joe.

Joe also needs to decide. In his decisions and priority setting, what is set before him is life or death, love or empty success. As with the others described in this chapter, Joe's decision will be paschal in nature. Whatever he says "yes" to implies a "no" to something or someone else. The greatest stranger in Joe's life lies within. He seems to be running from his feelings within, he is rendering Kathy and his children strangers. Often giving money and things is easier than giving of ourselves—our feelings, convictions, struggles, insecurities, vulnerabilities.

Emmaus as Model

The resurrection narratives in the Gospels are portraits of people who at first cannot recognize the Risen Lord. It is only gradually that the disciples came to see, recognize, and know. Specifically, in Luke's Emmaus account, the two disciples are so blinded by their loss and misery that they do not recognize Jesus. The stranger Jesus is recognized only when the two disciples and Jesus spend time with each other, talk with each other, share a meal with each other, and pray with each other. The three consciously attend to Scripture and tradition, the faith dimension of their lives, for meaning in the midst of desolation. Emmaus reminds us of the gradual nature of the process of recognizing the stranger: the stranger within, the stranger we once knew—and also God, the stranger. The Emmaus journey offers suggestions on how people in relationships can stem the process of emotional divorce.

God: The Stranger

Yes—God sometimes is the stranger. We can become blinded by the pain and difficulty of our lives. Not only do we sometimes fail to sense a loving God with us in the midst of our suffering, we sometimes operate out of a concept of God that suggests God is the cause of our trouble, the cause of our pain. Some of us have been raised with a punitive vision of God—that "God always gets his man." Someone recently told me that his younger brother was afflicted with sickness by God as a direct punishment for his (the older brother's) sins in his younger years. Easter faith, Emmaus faith, is the gradual "coming to see . . . recognize . . . and know that God through Jesus in the Spirit walks with us through our desolation and misery." He is not the cause of our pain; he is, rather, our companion in pain. The Spirit of Abba who hung with Jesus on the cross, the Spirit of Yahweh who went with European Jews into the showers, the same spirit walks with us in our various Emmaus journeys.

Often the recognition of God, the Stranger/Companion, is difficult to achieve. Often it can only happen through the mediation or influence of another person. In a recent address, national ministerial resource person Dolores Leckey said that we adults need to learn from adolescents who like to "hang around with each other." Though the influence of a negative peer group can be detrimental to adolescents, the positive side of such relationships is that the adolescents enjoy and often profit from being with each other. Religious institutions, parishes, and congregations would do well to teach the value of a non-churchy, ordinary, everyday, "being with each other" ministry. In being with each other, "faithing" with each other, and praying with each other, we help each other have the "jump of the imagination" that, despite appearances, always realizes that God loves us, walks with us, and as Paul says in Romans, works all things for the good of those that he loves.

CHAPTER TWO

Feeling Abandoned: The Core of Hurt

I guess I have not been privileged to counsel or help folks going through a mutually acceptable, no fault divorce. Most of the divorced people to whom I have ministered, often "after the fact" of the legal divorce, are terribly bruised by the entire process. For at least one of the two parties, a legal divorce is painful. Often such people have been caught off guard by his or her partner's dissatisfaction with the relationship and sense of urgency to get out of the commitment.

In his book *The Transforming Moment*, James Loder speaks of the primal experience of the toddler feeling abandoned by his or her parents as a feeling often seminally present in adult traumas. The point of Loder's study, however, is that often these break-down experiences can become break-through experiences or "transforming moments." Often adults I have seen "after the divorce" have displayed the feeling of being "abandoned children."

THE PURPLE RAINBOW

Abandonment: History Repeating Itself

One of life's paradoxes is that often a core conflict from childhood or early in life seems to clone itself, re-echo, or reverberate throughout our lives. Abandonment is one of those conflicts that I have seen people struggle with. After having been rejected or abandoned at least once, I think some people seek out people or relationships that will validate a poor self-image established by the first rejection. This self-image is often that one is unlovable and will ultimately be rejected again. It almost seemed that way with Penny, a lovely, spiritual woman in her late thirties, married almost twenty years, with three children. She had never known her father. He abandoned both her and her mother early in Penny's infancy. The early abandonment, the fantasized father, affected Penny's deep self. Despite the appearance of extraversion, happiness, and success, throughout her life there was an inner heaviness of spirit, a tendency to go deep within herself trying to find the inscrutable part of herself that her father could not love and she herself despised. It was Ed, her husband, who was always able to pull her out of the depths. He was her rock of stability, the man who shouted over the chasm of self doubt; "Penny, I love you; and I always will love you."

Then came Ed's turn for mid-life crisis. Exactly what happened, we still do not understand. All the familiar mid-life, male symptoms were there: a concern with body image, clothing, a heightened sexual appetite, though not necessarily the ability to perform, and an affinity for younger females. He resisted counseling or therapy, and

21

eventually left Penny for a younger woman. For weeks and months, Penny became the abandoned child. Again, "the why" of this rejection was as difficult to understand as her father's rejection. This one re-enforced a life conviction that she was indeed damaged goods. Penny went deeply into her own darkness.

Balancing Time On and Off the Cross

Penny's story reminds me of a life conviction of mine: we will indeed all spend time on the cross with Jesus. We need not seek out pain in life; life will provide us with quite enough, thank you. I do not say this as a pessimist or a spiritual masochist. Of those who ask "Why is there suffering in the world?", I have to ask "Why not?" Were any of us born with the guarantee that life would be struggle-free? From the pain of labor to the newborn child's birth trauma, life is peppered with struggle. The cross is inevitable.

The Jesus story reminds us over and over again that the cross is not the final chapter, nor the victor. Life, grace, resurrection will always break out and through the cross or death experiences. But neither can we run to the empty tomb. We cannot short-circuit the process. When the cross intervenes or intersects our lives, there are many feelings we can and will have, but there must be one overall response: trust in the God who draws us always to glory and new life. In Burt Bacharach's song *Raindrops Keep Falling On My Head*, B.J. Thomas sang some years ago, "The blues they sent to meet me, won't defeat me." In cross times we are entitled to all that Jesus experienced—tears, shouts, despair, feelings of abandonment. And we ought not to suppress or repress any of that. It is good to have a few women and John at the foot of the cross, or their equivalent coaxing us on. But the bottom line of Easter is that the cross will not defeat us.

And there are times, when we must in effect turn ourselves inside out. Instead of hanging motionless on the cross we should invert things, take the cross into our hearts and get out into the intersections of life.

The biographers of Martin Luther suggest now that he suffered from manic-depression, currently referred to as "bi-polar affective disorder." This disorder consists of periods of mania, times when a person has extremely high flung goals and is hyperactive, but also has times of depression, feelings of helplessness and hopelessness. Freud felt that the manic side of bipolar disorder disease was in fact the mind's attempt to smother or repress the chronic presence of depression. In that pre-psychological age, Luther devised his own therapeutic techniques for pulling himself out of depression. He would not just "hang on the cross," rather he would take the cross within him into life. Luther's advice to himself when depressed was:

—seek the company of others; do not remain isolated;
—discuss other matters, besides your depression;
—eat, drink, sing, joke, enjoy the company of the opposite sex;
—get angry and convert the anger into positive action;
—enjoy music: the devil cannot endure it;

—do not argue with the devil, that is, ignore morbid thoughts; treat them like nonsense;
—have faith in God, Jesus, the Holy Spirit.

Biographers believe that Luther placed great emphasis on the Pauline notion that we are saved by the life, death, and resurrection of Christ, because it enabled him to spiritually share in a victory already accomplished—the victory of life over death and morbidity. Luther is reported to have repeated over and over again during depressive episodes: "I have been baptized into Christ Jesus."

The Dark Night of the Soul
in the Face of Abandonment

With Penny, Martin Luther, and myself, the message of Easter (that the cross is not the ultimate victor) is a conviction that has "worked." Faith is a gift, and some seem more attuned to the gift, or able to use it, than others.

I have been with some for whom faith is not functioning as a therapeutic energy. In fact, this whole topic is not "clean," in the sense that even those of us who discover faith as a therapeutic energy, often go back and forth in it. It is the nature of faith to believe and not to believe. Faith consists of the "breathing in" of doubt and the "exhaling of trust and surrender." There are others, however, who experience what St. John of the Cross called "long, dark nights of the soul," times wherein the absence of God is felt more than the presence. Julie was such a woman.

24

THE PURPLE RAINBOW

Julie had experienced much abandonment as a child in an alcohol-abusing home. As is the case in many such environments, not much love or encouragement was shared in her family. She developed a relationship with a man, some years her senior, who provided stability for her during a terribly traumatic time of abandonment. Her sister died suddenly of alcohol-related causes. Julie and Paul married. She particularly loved to mother his two children from a previous marriage.

In a rather subdued discussion one evening, Julie raised some issues of dissatisfaction with the relationship. Her comments were non-indicting, really wondering about a kind of mutual culpability for some of their problems. Paul rather calmly responded that he too was dissatisfied, that he wanted out—now. He had found someone else that he wanted to be with. Within just a few days, Julie found herself in the midst of a nasty divorce. Paul worked out a settlement which financially left her to fend for herself. The relationship with Paul's two children was more or less severed. Within weeks, Julie was in a small rental apartment by herself.

Julie came to talk to me when she was on the mend. She had already endured months of deep depression and loneliness. I, in fact, was unaware of all that she was experiencing and had endured. She came to tell me, a pastoral counselor, what it felt like to be in the "dark night." She confessed that she wanted to die, that she in fact had contemplated suicide. During her darkest moments, she vacillated between being angry at God for having caused this pain, and confident that God, if he was at all loving, would understand her suicide.

Patrick J. Brennan

Julie spoke of how faith and Church did not work for her during her most desperate moments. She was either blaming God or expecting that he would erase blame if she escaped through self-destruction. Julie's self-predicting prophecy about her self-image, which she just continued to replicate over and over again throughout her lifetime, had come true again: she was abandoned. Since we always fashion our God concept out of pieces of what we feel and think about ourselves, she had created an image of God that would fit the abandonment motif. God had abandoned her, too. So had her Church, which, in her perception, did not welcome or include the divorced. She seemed no longer to fit in Church groups in which she and Paul had been "a couple."

Julie confessed that it was will power, a decision, an ethical imperative within, that kept her alive, not any feelings, not her faith. She then asked me to explain my understanding of God in such a difficult life situation.

God: The Cause or the Healer?

In my first assignment as a pastoral minister, I was asked to be the staff person for the baptismal preparation team. One of our first meetings involved a rather profound discussion about life, suffering, and the meaning of life. I said at one meeting that it was my experience that sometimes when God seems most obscure, absent, it is then that he is most present to us. I was told later that I had "lost" many of the members of the team. They could not quite understand what I had meant by that statement.

The late theologian Paul Tillich wrote of "the God above god." In that phrase he tried to explain this reality that confused the team. Often out of our personality types, or some other condition in our lives, we create a "God-image." The great challenge for those of us raised Catholic or Protestant is to check out whether our God-image is congruent with Revelation. Revelation demands that we reach beyond our gods, for the "God above god." In the diminishing, or absence of our impoverished notion of God, a fuller, richer experience of the "God above god" can begin to become present.

In short, I told Julie that in my experience God is not the cause of pain and suffering. It is the condition or situation of being a creature that we suffer, struggle, and die. God does not cause this. It is part of the evolution of creation. What, then, is the role of "the God above god" in suffering, hurt, or loss?

Revelation, Scripture, and tradition speak of God as the author of creation, a loving, but nonetheless just parent. Pain is the by-product of human growth and living. I can no longer blame God for hurt. "Bad things happen to good people." Perhaps this is part of the mystery of original sin, in which sin and struggle seem to be handed on from generation to generation.

God is not the cause of life's difficulties. Rather, God can be a reservoir of therapeutic healing and energy. I believe this was the God-experience of Jesus. Jesus grew to be able to confront the pain and ignominy of crucifixion, because—bottom line—he grew to understand God as his companion in pain rather than his adversary or cause of pain.

Julie: Now

Julie worships at the Eucharist daily now. The God and community that she had written off she has now come to re-interpret. She has come to see that God and community are not the sources of her pain. Rather pain happens. God and faith-filled relationships are present, there for us, to tap into, for healing, help, and meaning.

It has been Julie's experience that a God she had written off does care, and a community that she had written off does care. The experience of an unconditionally loving parent, and a loving community has led her back. Julie has met the God above god. Many so-called "inactive Catholics" would be "born again" if they experienced some of the love and meaning that Julie experiences now in her parish.

The Church Dropout Syndrome

Many of us who have done research in religious alienation have begun to notice a rather common pattern. Many who claim to have or had a "God story" or "Church story" of how God or Church has hurt them, as Julie did, have a cluster of other stories that have contributed toward pain and alienation in their lives. The God or Church story is simply the easiest to talk about and ventilate. Churches could spend time well in training people who have a concern for and understanding of the dropout syndrome.

I have experienced many people whose anger has been completely focused on their church of origin. The Church story has become an easy exit, an easy way to bury the pain of other life issues. Reconciliation with a community of faith becomes possible when the apparent enemy, the faith community, somehow reaches out in a posture of reach-out and story-listening. Such reach-out, story-listening ministry begins to lance wounds of bitterness and alienation that often people have created as a kind of "moat" around themselves, their deepest selves.

The Impasse Self

One of the mainstreams of contemporary psycho-therapy is the school of Gestalt therapy. Gestalt therapists seek to help name all that is going on both inside and outside of a client. Fritz Perls, the father of the movement, speaks of levels of personality. There is the first level, the cliché self, the most superficial layer of each of us. Then there is the role playing self—the job or vocation that each of us has—which often still insulates a deeper part of ourselves. It is an insulation that we create around the core self. Beyond the impasse self, according to Perls, is the implosive-explosive self, the experience of strong emotions, some expressed, some repressed or suppressed. The genuine self lies at the core of all of these layers of personality.

Often a person gets stopped, trapped, or stagnated at

the level of the impasse self. Often this is not conscious. It consists, however, of a person equivalently saying, "I do not want to hurt again, or anymore." Genuine peace-making or reconciliation requires that a person traverse the impasse self to begin to deal with the deeper level of the implosive-explosive self and the genuine self.

So Julie's obvious God story or God problem was a symbolic synthesis of many stories of abandonment, non-caring, and hurt. God and church were simply the easiest targets to focus on. We need to re-discover the God of miracles. By this I do not mean the god of showy, Cecil B. De Mille miracles whose transformations were really the craft of a cinematographer. Rather we need to re-discover the God of miracles who helps alcohol and substance abusers to abstain, those in the process of emotional divorce to struggle for reconciliation, those with low self-esteem to practice courage to be and become. Miracles still happen. God, however, has chosen a low profile these past two millenia. He is God the healer, not the problem causer.

Some people do not want quiet, subtle miracles or life transformations. Rather they want to clutch and hold on to their bad marriages, stress, or poor self-concept. Getting beyond the impasse self, we find ourselves in the desert, the dark night of the soul, the place of abandonment, where our genuine self can become wedded to God, our Abba.

John: A Man Abandoned

Often stories of relationships breaking apart, infidelity, and the experience of abandonment focus on the male

THE PURPLE RAINBOW

as aggressor or offender and the female as the victim. This, obviously, is not always the case: men experience the dark night of abandonment. John, like many men, was in fact emotionally absent during the first part of a 22-year marriage to Jane. As with many men, his first love was his career, and career-related dreams. This is a common form of non-sexual infidelity. His marriage was one of convention: it was the thing to do, the right time, the apparently right woman: Jane. Over the years Jane harbored resentment about the amount of time that his job demanded him to be away from the family, on the road. Jane's failure in this relational pattern was to not speak of it to her husband.

Rather than speak the truth, or communicate, she swept rage and resentment under an imaginary rug. None of us can do that. Emotions do not go away. They eventually must be dealt with. As Jane entered mid-life, with three young adult children raised, and a physical but not an emotional relationship with John, Jane began to find the problems under the rug to be insurmountable problems. But she found things that helped with these apparently insurmountable problems. She escaped from John and the marriage in a lucrative real estate career that she shaped for herself. She escaped also into graduate studies in psychology. At the institute where she studied, she developed a number of significant relationships—with men and women—that became a source of great sustenance for her. Her relationship with these people became much more satisfying and therefore more important to her than her relationship with John.

John is now having an awakening. The woman that he

had taken for granted, who had waited for a few precious moments of his time, had now found a life of her own —without him. One Saturday night, she confronted him with a brutally sobering announcement: she wanted a temporary separation. She had done her homework: she had an apartment; the one young adult son who was still at home had requested to come with her; she would continue to invest time and energy in real estate and graduate studies; she and John could see each other on occasions. She would spend time reflecting on what she wanted from the rest of her life, specifically whether she wanted to spend it with John.

What's A Man To Do?

The shoe was on a different foot now. He who for years had sped past a woman hungry for a relationship now found himself waiting and watching for someone speeding past him. He has sought the therapeutic advice of several of us in the vicinity of his residence. Our response has been common: wait, wait on her. "Wait, how long?", John wants to know. "We don't know," is our common reply. John and Jane's situation demands proactive counseling and therapeutic activities; but it also necessitates John's waiting as Jane has waited for him. Will there come a time of reconciliation, or of leaving each other? Yes. And in a community of discernment, we will know when the time has come. The temptation for a quick fix in these situations is great. A problem twenty years in the making is worth some time in the waiting, watching, hoping and fixing.

Adults Going Through Stages

"He/she is going through a stage," is a comment frequently made about children. The fact is, it applies with equal truth to adults. Emerging research shows that adults go through stages of growth, rest, then again spurts of growth. Research also shows that these stages are rarely experienced by men and women at the same time. When men are pursuing achievement, women are often in pursuit of intimacy and nurturing children or aging parents. When women begin to seek, to achieve, the male is often looking for yet-to-be-experienced intimacy. Women have stereotypically been the most patient in their capacity to "wait for men to grow, to go through a stage or stages." John's situation is a uniquely "end of the century" phenomenon. As patriarchy and sexism die a slow death, men are becoming aware that they must also reverence and wait for women as "they go through stages."

A psychologist wrote some years back that there would be fewer legal divorces in America if adults could only learn to wait on each other to go through stages. Part of Jane's absence may be repressed resentment expressing itself in revenge. The fact is both John and Jane have a lot invested in their marriage. In this day when 50% of American marriages end in divorce, and the statistics are even higher than that for second marriages, it would be

Patrick J. Brennan

good if counselors began to advise against quick solutions and "scratching every itch" for immediate satisfaction. We need to teach men and women to wait for each other.

John: Abandonment, Waiting, Impatience

As John modulates his demands and his expectations for a quick fix, Jane is beginning to see him anew. She expressed a desire recently to return. Those first signs of possible reconciliation made John want to demand an immediate return. "John," I would tell him, "wait. Face abandonment. Walk to the center of it. In the center of some forms of abandonment, love reaches purification, becomes sacrificial." Jane's potential return will be well worth waiting for resurrection. Powerless waiting, faith-filled waiting will also help to "close the door gently" if John and Jane discover they have grown completely apart from each other.

Abandonment: it resurfaces the primitive childhood fears we all have of being separated from our parents in a store or some other busy place. It re-echoes the birth trauma of being separated from our mother. But sometimes if waited out faithfully, with what Bernard Tyrell calls "the will to discomfort," the uncomfortable abandonment, willfully accepted, introduces us to the One who will never abandon us.

CHAPTER THREE

Best Friends: Left Behind

It was a damp, gray fall Tuesday afternoon. I was finishing an afternoon of reflection with senior citizens. As I walked from the meeting place to the vestibule, to greet the people who had attended the afternoon, an elderly man, slight in build, walked up to me. He was in his late seventies. Jack was his name. "Can I see you for a minute," he asked. "Sure," I responded. "My name is Jack, and they're all telling me I need counseling. Maybe I'm going crazy." With that he broke down, and began sobbing. He pulled a large, already well-used handkerchief from his back pocket. He cried into the handkerchief for a few moments. I turned him and myself away from the crowd and walked slowly to a quiet place.

Jack told his story. He never knew why, but his mother and father dropped him and his sister off at an orphanage, when he was five and she was seven. Eventually they were separated, as they passed from foster home to foster home. He suspected the reason for their parents leaving them was poverty. Jack finally got out on his own, held a job for awhile, and then served in the Army in the Second World War. When he was discharged, he returned to the work force, and took a small apartment. In the apartment building, he became acquainted with a young woman, who had a baby. She had no husband. Jack and Elizabeth became "small talk" friends. She grew to trust him enough to tell him her story. She was an unwed mother. The father of the child, a little girl, did not want to be married. She did not know where he was now.

Jack was already in his thirties in 1943, and he was anxious to be married. He began to care for Elizabeth and Mary, the baby, as his own. Within a year and a half, they were married. Jack adopted Mary legally. He and Elizabeth went on to have their own son and daughter. When she was about twenty-five years of age, Mary, Elizabeth's daughter by another man, contracted cancer. It was terminal. Elizabeth found herself in the unexpected position of nursing the young woman she had given life to. She agonized with Jack, in private, over Mary's suffering, and eventual death. She kept asking why? and how? Yet her struggle, private or with Jack, was left behind when she was with Mary. She was only courage, love, and faith with Mary. Through it all, Jack mourned Mary's gradual passing, too. But his greater pain was to watch his wife suffer through the loss of her daughter. He loved to care for and remove any pain from Elizabeth's and Mary's lives, but in this situation, he was powerless. Toward the middle of his life, Jack began to deal with the mystery of powerlessness in the face of some of life's hurts.

Elizabeth carried the death of her daughter with her for the rest of her life. Though she and Jack went on to raise the other two children, she continually felt Mary's death was the result of the child being born out of wedlock. Time marched on. The son and daughter grew up, got married, raised families of their own. While they tried to offer aid to their aging parents, Elizabeth felt that this too was an example of the tragic nature of life, that the children, busy with their own lives, really did not have time for their parents.

Elizabeth's health broke down. She suffered a severe heart attack, and then a fall down a step into the garage shattered parts of her osteoparosis-filled frame. Jack, by this time, had developed kidney disease and regularly had to go for dialysis. Yet the story of Jack is a story of maximum sacrificial love. Jack loved Elizabeth, in her emotional and physical broken condition even more than when she was whole. He spent his retirement as well as his own physical, therapeutic process, caring for her.

In our time with each other, after Elizabeth's death, Jack would pull out the large napkin-like handkerchief over and over again as he talked of his deceased wife. In the last twenty-five or thirty years of his life, he was the caretaker of his wife, her nurse, confidant, and minister. Even his own afflictions did not stop him from giving all to and for her. Now, in her absence, he was in an almost adolescent type of crisis. To the degree he could no longer care for her and his family, he no longer knew who he was. Some writers with a greater analytical, clinical mind and background than mine might rather quickly diagnose Jack as someone with incredibly low self-esteem who found his self-worth in pleasing other people. Why in this age of the self, could he not use his widower-retirement years for the things he never got to do because of marital-familial commitments? Perhaps the answer lies not so much in a neurotic diagnosis as in a spiritual one. Jack's life seems to have been a response to the loneliness, pain, and abandonment that reaches back close to eighty years when his sister and he were left at an orphanage and then separated from each other through a series of foster placements. In a real sense, Jack, though he could not verbally describe himself in this way, was ministering out of his own pain. He knew ache in its deepest form. Because he endured it much, he was attracted to it in others, and tried as no one had with him, to eradicate as much of it as he could.

Those "large handkerchief" experiences in my office were not moments of identity crisis. They were rather a married man who had lost his best friend, a true minister who had lost his congregation, a man often crushed himself who now was faced with the depths of his lifelong personal suffering. Naively I offered superficial antidotes: How about getting involved in senior citizen functions at the parish? How about buying a pet for companionship? How about lining up specific vacation time with each of the married children? Some he accepted, others, like the pet, he rejected out of hand because "Elizabeth would not allow any pets around the house." She was still clearly a living reality for him. No, Jack had entered

THE PURPLE RAINBOW

"the greatest suffering," something that each of us has faced or will face: the entrance into the greatest unique pain for each of us. For Jack it was the absence of his best friend, whom he tended to with a true sacrificial love, and the confrontation with his own lifelong woundedness.

Finally the solution came, the healing came. I received a call that Jack had died of his chronic kidney disease. Healing? How could death be a healing? Because there was clearly no mortal, human antidote to Jack's distress. He was longing for two realities: communion with his beloved friend, and oneness with the ultimate healing power of the divine presence. At Jack's funeral homily, I offered him congratulations—congratulations at passing on to those two ultimate realities that he so longed for. Some older people can, I believe, die on purpose—especially if their emotional condition is connected with some other physical condition. A strong will or commitment to others and/or God, can throw the human system into over-drive to compensate for the organ inferiority. But then, without the meaning found in love or service, the reason to live is no longer as strong as the reason to die. Trusting in who and what waits on the other side of death, some seniors let go into the inevitable: the reality of brokenness and death. It is not a suicidal act; rather it is a ceasing of the resistance to the inevitable.

Jack's funeral liturgy was a celebration of resurrection. On the one hand, Jack had always served out of the cross experiences of his life, trying to ease the pain in others that he was so familiar with in himself. On the other hand, he had moved on to another dimension of reality—a new age, a new time, a new Presence, that alone could heal "the greatest suffering."

On Being Widowed: Building Again

I know senior widowed people; and I know people who have lost their spouse in their early forties. Especially when such lightening strikes a good, loving relationship, the death experience causes all of us to reflect on the quality of relationships in our lives—especially ones that we have not tended to, or we have allowed to deteriorate. Healthy love abruptly ended causes irresponsible, immature love to do some critical analysis.

But being a widow or widower is not all spiritual heroics, martyrdom, or witnessing. It is a process of grief and recovery that involves the natural stages of grief and recovery documented by Dr. Elizabeth Kubler-Ross. It can also be a time of a rage that is greater than anger —anger at God, if one's God-concept sees God as author of pain rather than healing; anger and rage at the beloved who has left suddenly, abruptly. The one left behind needs to recover, to build a life again, even to parent children—all with the unexpected, unwanted loss of one's spouse.

On Bruno and Esther

Two stories of older men are good examples of the *elan vital*, the life force, present in the widowed, seeking out life and love again—indeed, in any of us who have died and want to rise again.

THE PURPLE RAINBOW

Bruno was an elderly man of Polish heritage. He had been widowed for about seven years. He assumed a retreating posture relative to life. He no longer worked, so he busied himself all day with domestic and garden chores around the large home he had shared for years with his wife and children. He ate a sparse supper around 4:30 pm or 5:00 pm and then went to bed around 6:30 pm. In bed, he read or watched "pure, clean" TV reruns till he fell asleep. Obviously his internal clock woke him at about 3:00 am every morning. He would lie in bed for a couple of hours waiting for the sun to rise and the alarm to go off, calling him to daily mass. He repeated this ritual for about six years. Then, on an annual trip south to a Florida town where his daughter and son had relocated, the daughter's next door neighbor intruded into his life.

An elderly widow herself, Esther did not abide by typical expectations, or stereotypes regarding male-female relationships. She found Bruno to be a good, appealing man. She invited him out to dinner. Though Bruno was Catholic, he enjoyed going to the services at her Baptist church. After seeing each other for several weeks during the extended winter vacation, they began to talk about the possibility of living with each other forever in marriage.

Bruno came to me with a curious request. Reflecting a deep belief in the Communion of Saints, a Catholic tradition that the spirits of the deceased are alive with the Holy Spirit, Bruno asked me, "Do you think my deceased wife, Margaret, would be offended in heaven if I took another woman as my wife?" I asked Bruno to talk

41

a little about how Esther had influenced his life. He reflected on his previous retreating posture. He could now see the early dinner—early bed—early waking—early rising syndrome as symptomatic of great loneliness. "I am so lonely," he said, "I have been getting by, but I guess I want more out of life."

"Bruno, knowing how much your wife loved you, I am sure she would want you to be as happy as possible until you all meet again in eternal life," I said. "If you and Esther love each other, I would go for it!"

Bruno obviously evidenced glorified wounds. The loss of Margaret was still a wound, but that wound was beginning to become a part of a re-born glorified reality—the new oneness in love Bruno found with Esther. They married in September. He died the following May. Both he and Esther knew that he had a chronic, potentially fatal disease. This did not blind them to the months of joy that they could have with each other—months they had anticipated with hope. Bruno and Esther, both widowed, were permanently wounded by death in their first marriages. But they felt called beyond the trappings of death to new life and love together at an advanced age.

On Liam and Carmen

Liam was born in Ireland. He had a varied career here in America, including working in vaudeville during its heyday in New York City. But it was in Chicago that he met the love of his life, Carmen. Though in their sixties when the Catholic Church's Second Vatican Council came in the 1960s, they embraced the changes and became extremely active in many of the ministries open to them, especially pastoral care of the sick. Carmen became sick with chronic heart disease as they both passed into their seventies. Though she became minimally limited, they both continued their activity in social and ministerial lifestyles.

Carmen died suddenly of heart failure one night. At Carmen's funeral, Liam, a daily communicant, broke into my homily several times to agree about the remarkable attributes of his wife. He also broke into the general intercessions, praying aloud in praise and thanksgiving for the gift of Carmen.

Most touching was the final commendation at the cemetary. Liam bent down and kissed the part of the coffin over Carmen's face. Kissing her through the barriers of death, he said, "Good-bye my love; I will see you again soon." Liam began a grieving period. He continued his ministerial activity, but it did not satisfy him. With the absence of Carmen, there was almost a physical appendage removed.

Months later, he met an old childhood sweetheart; their young romance had been one of those true love things that somehow does not work out. Dating and courtship began, reluctantly, at first. How could romance happen again for two widowed people in their eighties? Liam and his re-discovered love, Eve, are witnesses to the reality and possibility of romance, commitment, and sexuality in the senior years. With the graying of America, they are reminders to us that contemporary seniors will not be bound by the shackles of senior citizen stereotypes.

Patrick J. Brennan

As with many mentioned in this book, the therapeutic energy for Liam's and Eve's grief process was and is faith. At a daily visitation to his local church for prayer in the Eucharistic chapel, Liam's struggle with his wound of grief and his guilt at being lonely and simultaneously in love, reached a climax before the Eucharistic presence of Jesus. At one moment, he looked through tears at the crucifix—the paradigmatic artistic statement about all human woundedness. Suddenly, Liam's faith saw the head of Carmen on the crucified body of Jesus. She looked at her husband, says Liam, and smiled and nodded yes to Liam's prayerful struggle about taking Eve as his second wife.

It is interesting that the cross, as a symbol, should become the vehicle for communicating good news of new life, and new beginnings. At times, folks have commented that perhaps I write and speak too much about the cross. I think the comments reflect a shallow understanding of the cross as part of the paschal mystery. There is no beginning and end in death and resurrection. Often the experience of resurrection intersects with the experience of death. It is in the struggle that new life begins. What is spoken of as the original Easter experience actually began with Jesus' hours on the Good Friday cross.

Faith is a way of seeing, John's Gospel tells us over and over again. Liam saw Carmen his deceased wife, as prophet of truth, as still alive, intersecting with the crucified body of Christ. In death, Liam's faith saw new life.

Liam and Eve married recently and moved to a warmer

44

climate in a southern state. Bruno, Esther, Liam, and Eve—and the two who were called home, Margaret and Carmen—are witnesses to the possibility that the greatest suffering experienced in faith can be transformed by the power of God into glorified wounds.

Faith in the Midst of Loss

One characteristic of all those involved in the stories in this chapter was and is faith. I run the risk in talking about faith this way to lead people to think that faith is a kind of magical eraser that removes pain. The grief of all widows and widowers discussed in this section was not removed by their relationship with God. Faith was and is a belief/hope/conviction, that life will be victorious over death. Faith was and is a relationship with a personal God, a relationship that suggests that there is meaning even in suffering. Faith was and is for these people a way of life, doing, getting on with life even in the midst of pain.

A question that all of this poses for us is what are we to do with a widowed person who does not have this apparent faith. I believe that a reliable, consistent, committed presence with, for, and to such a grieving person is the best gift we can offer. If faith values and realities can seep through to the other person—either in prayer or general conversation, we have performed a genuine ministry. We may awaken the faith already within the person. Obvious talk about God and religion or God's plan often does not work in situations of loss.

CHAPTER FOUR

Jilted!

Some of the lectionary readings about the rejection that Jesus experienced from some people particularly disturbed me this year. I think that is because I have spent so much time this year counseling people who have been hurt in love relationships—the pre-marital, but "planning to be married soon" kind of relationships.

I have seen more young women who have experienced this kind of struggle than young men who have. Yet I know it happens to both men and women. There has been a spate of research lately into why this phenomenon occurs—people on the verge of commitment suddenly coming "uncoupled." Much of the research has involved a kind of "male bashing." Why do relationships break up? It is because of: *Women Who Love Too Much; Smart Women, Foolish Choices; Men Who Can't Love; Male Commitmentaphobia,* and on and on.

In this reflective book, we will not spend much time on the causality of young couples splitting apart. In fact, some of the dynamics of pre-married couples breaking up are probably similar to those of the already married discussed in the first chapter on "becoming strangers." I would rather reflect on the paschal journey, the journey toward new life that recovering from such a loss can be. It must be noted that such an experience can also be one that results in severe devastation, stagnation, or retardation socially, emotionally, and spiritually. Not just the healing power of God, but that joined to effective use of mind and will and faith-filled, therapeutic relationships usually result in growth and recovery. The Beginning Experience, a weekend for the recently divorced, describes the goal of recovery for those "jilted" as well as those divorced: to be able to close the door gently on the previous relationship.

Geri: A Case Study

Geri fell in love with Marty when she was in her early twenties. He confessed that the same happened to him, though his behavior did not indicate it. This might be a good principle to articulate here: the best prediction of future behavior is present behavior. Occasionally I hear engaged people talk of being able to change their partner in the future. It has been my experience in both personal relationships and in helping others that most of us can only effectively change one person—the self. Marty's words were those of love, futuring, and commitment. His behavior was that of self-centeredness, rebellion against commitment, and a disdain for women. He cancelled dates, came late for commitments, would abruptly stop talking on some evenings with Geri, call several times a day every day, then not call for weeks.

The victim, perhaps needless psychological martyr, through this whole ordeal was Geri, who was both *in love* and *loved* Marty. She accepted his inconsistent behavior, forgave and began again multiple times; accepted the inexplicable parentheses of time between visits and phone calls, and even financially supported him through long years of vocational searching and pining. Geri's family began to sour on the prospects of her future with Marty; so did her friends. But love is blind, and she persisted in the relationship with relentless passion.

The end came abruptly. Two years ago, they made rather specific plans for marriage. One month later Marty announced he would never marry Geri or any woman. Geri, with the feeling of emotional rape, begged for reasons. He gave none. After six years of a relationship that was almost at an engagement stage, Marty stepped out of her life, never to be seen again. An attempt to contact him several months later to check on his well-being was met by a verbal rebuff: Geri was not to initiate contact again.

The young man's erratic behavior strongly suggests pathology to me. But discussing his pathology, how unhappy the union would have been, how it would probably have ended in divorce, all did little to ease the woundedness Geri felt so profoundly. Had Marty been more honest and at least offered a reason why: sexual identity confusion, a call to celibacy, whatever, the blow to Geri's ego would have been less. In this situation, however, she was left only to ruminate on how she caused the split; it must have been some failing in her.

As with most people in a situation of grief, Geri was and still is going through flip-flops—denial, anger, bargaining, acceptance, and deep loneliness and depression. As a helper, all I or others can do is be with, "faith with," and pray with her.

I remember one day in my office, Geri sobbing: "Why did he do this?" My impotent reply was, "I don't know!" Geri was into her "greatest suffering." The man she loved the most, wanted the most, loved most sacrificially, had walked out on her. He left her after verbal promises of marriage and children. She was already "married in her head." Why did he do it? As with most suffering, there is no answer to that question of "Why?" There is, however, opportunity: the opportunity for the Job experience. Job eventually gave up on the question "why?" because he began to intuit that through the struggle he was moving from a God of hearsay to a God he knew personally and sensed was with him.

Rebounds That Deny the Reality of Grief

With Geri somewhat, and more with other young women, I have seen attempts to deny, cover up, suppress the reality of deep hurt and woundedness. This is most often done by quickly jumping to other relationships. The idea seems to be: if someone else finds me attractive, then I must really be; my "ex" was really mistaken. Perhaps too often what leads some women into such problematic relationships with attractive, but uncommitted young men, is a radical doubt about their own self-worth.

Maybe what Geri and others similar to her must learn is that no other person can do for us what only we ourselves can do, that is: learn healthy self-love and self-esteem. Healthy self-love, self-esteem prepares a young man or woman to enter a relationship with the self concept of an equal. Without self-esteem, or by looking for it in another, the person lacking it sets up a superiority-inferiority disparity that will never permit a healthy adult relationship to grow.

Jumping quickly to another relationship provides some immediate gratification. But in the long run it can be problematic, because of unfinished business—the unfinished business of inner healing and growth.

Barroom Wisdom

While on vacation with friends recently, I rather abruptly decided to curtail my time at a vacation spot and return to work. All my guests were to leave that evening, and I was feeling an ominous discomfort. "Why don't you stay on," challenged one of my friends. "No," I said, "I've had enough food, drink, and sun." "That's not it," said the friend. "There's something on your mind. If you were to stay alone, you'd have to deal with it and you don't want to. Have you ever noticed how people in bars look all over the room for the first two drinks. But on the third, they stare into the mirror behind the bar. The booze gives them the false courage to look at themselves. You don't need the false courage of liquor.

But I sense you do need to look at and within yourself, alone.''

I was caught. Like a child, I gave a smile of recognition at being caught. He was exactly on target. I did not want to be alone, because I did not want to deal deeply with the mystery, the inner workings of me.

So it is often with a number of people who have been hurt. There is a desire to deny the hurt, anesthetize the hurt, run from the hurt. But paradoxically, it only gets better when you begin to enter into it, enter into what James Loder calls ''the void.''

Implosive Therapy

We do not understand the process completely, but healing happens in part through verbalization and emotional catharsis, or emptying. Geri and others do well to enter into all the hurting feelings that they have, feel them powerfully, talk about them with trusted others, and cry much. They need to release tears of hurt, tears of rage, tears of humiliation. Without such an emotional release, there is a danger that all of that negative emotional energy will be turned inward, which is what some forms of depression are made up of. This is called by some ''implosive therapy.'' It refers to entering fully into the pain, letting all the feelings come, not being afraid of them and having the courage to admit the profundity of the hurt.

I think this ought not be done once, but as many times as is needed. While part of it needs to be done alone, it is good also to have direction and mentoring during this phase of the grieving/healing process. Part of the "entering the pain" process can be committing the broken pieces of one's life to the mercy of God, in prayer. Repetitive prayer for healing leads to some experiences of transformation. God gives "good things" to those who pray, says Jesus in Matthew. He gives the Spirit to those who pray, says Jesus in Luke.

Learning To Trust Again

While quick-fix, rebound relationships are often part of the syndrome of recovering from the loss of a love, such relationships do not necessarily include the presence of trust in relationships again. Trust is the hardest thing to learn again. But, again, those hurt in love do themselves a disservice when they practice distancing behaviors between themselves and others. Trust refers to slowly giving one's heart, one's inner world, to another person, when the person's words and actions reveal that he or she is worthy of such a precious gift from the self. Understanding, trusting again—learning to give that inner core to someone—is extremely difficult. Each of us constructs a protective structure around our fragile egos after we have been hurt. That is probably good for a time. But there comes a time in the healing process when it becomes toxic to maintain those distancing behaviors.

To maintain mistrust is to revert to a period of infant development. Erik Erikson taught us years ago that the infant cannot move on to become a healthy baby child, adolescent, and adult until and unless he or she learns to

THE PURPLE RAINBOW

trust the relational world around him or her. Chronic mistrust is a kind of inner paralysis, a subdued cynicism about the nature of life and relationships. Failure to open up again in a loving, trusting relationship robs one of that which we are all in need of: love and friendship.

Geri and others like her need to take small steps toward learning to trust again. Without turning a new "significant other" into a therapist, she and others need to explain the difficulty that they have in trusting, how they are trying to do it in their own time, and that they need some coaxing and encouragement in coming to trust again.

Don't Kill the Butterfly

The antithesis of what we discussed above is the hurting person or a new significant other trying to hasten the trusting process. An old Russian fable tells the story of someone who tore open a caterpillar in a cocoon in an attempt to find the butterfly. Obviously life in all forms—caterpillar or butterfly—was lost in the man's eagerness for the end product. So it is with trusting again. It comes gradually. It comes with practice. It cannot be forced.

One of the experiences that can serve as pseudo-trust is premature sexual activity. Until the AIDS crisis hit, we went through fifteen or twenty years in which love was equated with genital sexual experiences, or warm feelings or attraction were declared as license for it. The recovering person can be further traumatized by premature sexual activity, either precipitously self-initiated, or demanded by another.

Patrick J. Brennan

Unlike the sexuality packaged by the media as a frivolous, spontaneous thing, true sexuality is at the heart of who we are as persons. To begin to relate to another person on a genital-sexual level is to begin to offer one's total self to another. Specifically, intercourse ought to be the act of the greatest co-operation, communication, intimacy, and commitment. For a person learning to trust again to enter these deep waters too quickly is to court deeper depression and potential hurt.

The Importance of Rituals of Good-Bye

Pictures, gifts, notes, letters from loved ones are treasured objects that we hold onto. They almost become sacraments that help us feel "the real presence of another," when that person is far away or perhaps deceased. While these mementos are life-giving when the person is a significant, contributing part of our life—past or present, such objects become reminders of heartache and pain when they were given by the person who left, dropped the relationship, or otherwise was unfaithful. When the time is right, experience has shown that symbolic rituals of letting go of the other person can be helpful. This includes things like burning, burying, casting in the lake, river, or ocean those mementos of the relationship, that reactivate hurting memories. Note: these are not rituals of hostility, but rather rituals of healing, liberation—almost exorcism. Symbolically the recovering person is "letting go" of the relationship, "letting go" of the past—burying false hope that things might again be as they once were.

In discussing such rituals with a young woman who was in the midst of such a process, she wisely reminded me that such rituals do not remove the woundedness. This is, of course, true and points to the vision of this book. As we rise from suffering and death to new life, we are certainly glorified—but we are still wounded. Many such wounds or marks we will carry with us for the rest of our lives.

Enemy Love: The Process Coming Full Circle

One of the signs of deep conversion, in the teaching of Jesus, as portrayed by the Gospel writers, is the ability to pray for one's enemies, for those who have hurt us. To pray for one who has hurt us goes against human nature. It can only be done through divine help. It can happen for most folks only after a period of healing, and spiritual-emotional pastoral care. One of the signs of someone "jilted" really being on the mend is the ability to pray for the well-being, the healing, the health and the happiness of the person who has hurt us. Again here we have to guard against the premature "caterpillar syndrome." To do "enemy love" prematurely could exacerbate one's own melancholia, denying the hurt and anger one really feels and frustrating the necessary implosion that we discussed earlier. But if many of the steps discussed previously are taken properly, one may very well find oneself in the position of renewed strength that permits seeing the offender in a new light, as a vulnerable, sinful, hurt and hurting person—in need of the same power that has helped transform the wounds of the jilted: the love of God.

So hang in there, Geris of the world. When you think you are about to fall off the edge, you must remember God made the world round and with gravity. There are no edges to fall from.

CHAPTER FIVE

Parenting Your Parents

She had not felt good for several days. She explained it away, however, as a recurrence of an old kidney infection. What my mother did not tell my father, my brother, or me was that she also had great difficulty at night with her breathing when she would lie down in bed. After about four days of the labored breathing, she could no longer take it. My father called early one morning and asked me to come home and drive my mother to the hospital. I consented, none of us realizing the deep difficulties we were really in the midst of.

My mother was breathing heavily when I arrived. She had a pasty, sweaty look on her face. As we travelled to the hospital in which my family has the most confidence, my mother asked me to go faster. That was quite unlike her, who usually advocates taking 25 m.p.h. side streets to whatever the destination. My speed and anxiety accelerated. When we arrived at the emergency room, I was met by a nurse friend of mine. She quietly commented to me "she does not look good." My mother was taken from us and moved behind the scenes for diagnosis. An hour elapsed. My brother and aunts arrived, all seeking information that I did not have. Finally, a doctor emerged from behind the scenes. He gave us the truth. "She is in congestive heart failure."

"Jesus!" I said aloud. I dug my fingernails into my hands. For a variety of reasons and for many years, I have served as the caretaker of my family, making sure everyone was happy, healthy, O.K. I was always in charge, in control. As with so many people whose stories are told in this book, I suddenly felt powerless. The "father" used to being in charge, I became child-like in the hands of the doctor.

"Will she be all right?" I asked.

"We think so," explained the doctor, "but we have to find out what caused this to happen."

I have since come to understand congestive heart failure as a largely symptomatic disorder that arises from some other dysfunction—either of the heart or some other organ. The heart's performance simply cannot adequately deal with the reality of what is happening to the body, and the lungs fill up with fluid. Untreated, a patient would literally drown in his or her own fluids.

My mother was transferred to cardiac intensive care, where her lungs were drained and her condition was as stabilized as it could be. Throughout the long days of diagnosis and testing, I resembled the detective Columbo, running after medical personnel seeking out answers, information, a sense of the future. None was forthcoming, not immediately. I had to wait.

THE PURPLE RAINBOW

My mother resembled a frightened child in the hospital. She had been the strong one in the family—the perpetual nurturer of the more vulnerable males she lived with and to whom she gave life. The electronic equipment, the doctors, the nurses created a strange, frightening world for her. She feared the nights especially. She wanted me to spend the night in the hospital. Of course, I consented. What began was a long week of sleeping between two chairs in the visitor's lounge, assuring my mother of my presence before she went to sleep and when she woke, returning home to get cleaned up, and then attempting to get a few hours of work done before I returned to the hospital.

The cardiologist eventually told us of her disorder: mytrostenosis, a narrowing of one of the valves of the heart, incubating in her since a childhood bout with rheumatic fever. Prognosis: fair to good. Medication would be tried first, if that did not work down the line, something else like surgery or angioplasty (balloon therapy) might be required.

A week that seemed like a month came to an end, and my mother was released. I had to arrange home nursing care before she left the hospital. During her stay in the hospital, my father had asked me to come home one evening, too, because he felt flu-like. I told him I could not handle both cases simultaneously, that my brother, aunts, or someone else would have to help him. I felt curt, abrupt—but also torn in two. I could do no more. As I helped my mother into the house upon her return, I had to help her with everything. She had no strength in her legs to climb the stairs. I had to more or less carry her in.

Patrick J. Brennan

During the days in the hospital, and the ensuing days at home, I looked at the woman who days before had been everyone's tower of strength. Now heavily medicated on strong substances her body was not used to, she would doze away in the midst of conversation. I stared at her one night, when she slipped away in mid-conversation and tears rolled down my cheeks. Where was the woman I once knew, the strong maternal figure I once had? Though I was in my late thirties at the time, I was almost crying out for a mother. Maybe I was also realizing that the little lady who dozed off on me now was becoming my child.

Spiritual Surrender

Two weeks into my mother's convalescence at home, I was beginning to feel that things were forever altered, but we were nonetheless getting back to some normalcy. I moved back to the rectory, after spending a few days assisting my father and the visiting nurse in caring for my mother. The visiting nurse warned me one day: "Watch out for flu or pneumonia. These conditions easily aggravate tendencies toward a recurrence of heart failure."

A few days later, the phone range early. "Come home," my father said, "your mother is vomiting and has a fever." In such circumstances, one easily recedes into primitive spirituality: "How could you, God. How could you allow my worst fear to be actualized. She has the flu!"

For most of the day, I held a bucket into which my mother wretched. We called the nurse, who called the doctor, who prescribed new medicines. The nurse

60

warned me, "Watch out for 103° fever—that's a danger point for these patients." Things got better in terms of symptoms for a couple of days. I returned to work. One late afternoon, the office phone range. Again it was my father, himself a struggling senior citizen. "Your mother's fever has gone up to 103°. Come home!"

I had to cancel my umpteenth meeting or appointment to get quickly from downtown Chicago to home on the southside. For some reason I had a great morbidity about this turn of events. The nurse's words, "Watch out for 103° fever," haunted me. My muted hysteria throughout this whole experience was due to the very close bond I have had with my mother. I had been a sickly child, with asthma and other problems. She transported me to doctors. Throughout my lifetime I always tried to reciprocate by watching out for her—even in childhood. If I had been the family caretaker, I especially was her caretaker.

Now reality was settling in. She was not mine. I did not and could not control her life or her death. I feared this ride home, and asked my associate if she would ride with me. Wisely she pointed out that she should stay by the phone in case the doctor called. I walked into the winter night, got in my car in the parking lot, filled with fear and dread. My mind searched for a way to approach this awful ride home. I landed on one that had worked for me for years, a prayer that I had learned from a spiritual director while I was in graduate theology school. I talked about this prayer in another book, *Spirituality for an Anxious Age*. It was an articulation of my primary adult conversion experience as I battled emotional problems in my early twenties. The prayer is, "Father, into Your

Hands, I hand over my life,'' a derivation of Jesus' dying words on the cross in Luke 23:46, actually also a re-echoing of Psalm 31:6. Praying that prayer in repetitive-mantra like style had turned my mind from fear to trust many years ago. It continues to be my "maintenance prayer" for inner peace.

With no real resources left, I fell back on the prayer as I drove to my parents' home. I changed the words: "Father, into Your Hands, I hand over her life." What was I doing? I was surrendering control over my mother, placing her in the loving hands of God. I wanted her to live, but I was and am convinced that even in death there is One who loves her more than I—Abba, God the Creator-Parent. "Father, into Your Hands I hand over her life." I prayed for the forty-minute ride home. I entered their home, a place filled with the ambiguity of life and death, with a deep sense of inner peace.

In Between Times

The greatest challenge that I experienced in my mid-life caring for senior parents was striking a balance between my own willfulness and directedness (control) and surrender. That first acute crisis with my mother was followed rather quickly by:

—a 3:00 a.m. call to another hospital where my father had to be treated for acute asthma and emphysema;
—a 3½ day hospitalization of my father for more lung problems, complicated by acute gouty arthritis;
—3 surgeries on my father for skin cancer;

—extensive bone marrow and scanning tests looking for deeper cancers;

—a broncho-spasm that resulted in a heart attack which resulted in my father's degeneration into heart failure;

—a recent hospital stay for my mother due to recurring broken vertebrae.

(Though his body seems stronger than my mother's, the assaults on my father have been more repetitive and apparently ravaging.)

During one emergency admission of my father, as the secretary asked for vital information, I felt like crying. This time I felt like crying not just for him and my mother who suffers with him. I felt like crying for myself. I had grown tired of the constant hospitalizations, the uncertainty of what would happen, the constant adaptation of my lifestyle to be of more help. Tears wanted to come another time when a hospital chaplain, a brother, approached me as I waited for an elevator. He said, "You know, we on the pastoral staff are worried about you."

I resisted his ministry with, "Oh, I'm doing just fine." Part of me, though, wanted to tearfully confess utter fatigue. I reserved my ache for a spiritual director-therapist who is most often representative of the faith community for me—my mentor.

Some Principles I Have Learned

Redemption occurs in part when we put our stories of life, death, and resurrection at the service of brothers and sisters also on the journey; and we learn from each other. That is the reason I am sharing this rather personal odyssey with you.

Advances in medicine have greatly increased the life expectancy of Americans. The projections as to the number of people who will survive into their eighties, nineties, and hundreds increase regularly. Never before will so many of us in the middle period of our lives be responsible for nurturing two other age groups: our children and our parents. I felt both this privilege and tension recently on a vacation when both my six-year-old niece and my mother were left in my care. I felt extremely tense, in these isolated situations, caring for the both of them. Yet, I was only feeling in microcosm what many of us may feel over years: responsibility for two generations other than our own.

I would like to share some principles that have come to me over the years. I share it as very flawed wisdom, for I indeed struggle in trying to live the wisdom inherent in it. Much of it has been taught to me by others who also deal with this phenomenon.

(1) In caring for your parents, it is easy for some to be directed too much by pseudo-guilt, false guilt, that even more could and should be done for them.

(2) A caring adult child does not try to be/do all for the parent(s). He/she becomes aware of the many types of new resource people in the emerging industry of gerontology. As adult children we can become bridges to people like home nurses and to organizations like "Meals

on Wheels.'' We ought not get into the habit of doing it all ourselves.

(3) Without some limits put on responding to a senior's needs, these needs can become fast-working quicksand, which soon overcomes the son or daughter. A son or daughter needs to maintain his/her own life.

(4) Parents need to maintain their sense of self-worth and independence. To the degree a problem is not life-threatening, seniors ought to be encouraged to do for themselves.

(5) Seniors are people, with wisdom, thoughts, feelings —and a need to communicate, not just to be nursed and cared for.

(6) Some seniors, especially those with broken health, can get moody because they sense they cannot be or do, as they did in the past. That moodiness ought not be argued with, but rather empathized with and understood. Sometimes silence is the better response to crabbiness or moodiness than is rationality or arguments.

(7) While consultation with our parents is necessary, neither approval nor permission is needed in every circumstance wherein we as adults feel that we are creating the most life-giving situation. A case in point is an elderly couple I know who always resisted air conditioning in their home. The horrendously hot summers of the late 1980s wreaked havoc on their lungs, hearts, and arthritic

limbs. Finally, the adult children decided they no longer needed permission. They acted, and had central air conditioning installed. The parents' condition improved markedly.

(8) Avoid morbidity. Sometimes in dealing with our parents, we see only death and decline, rather than the joy, life, humor, and the presence of God still alive within them.

(9) Live a spirit of "into Your Hands." Realize that much of what we are experiencing in aging parents is indeed out of our hands. The mysteries of aging, sickness, and death are ones toward which we must confess some degree of powerlessness.

(10) Mid-lifer, care for your own health! The mid-thirties begins the decline of a person's physical ability. This decline necessitates a regimen of spirituality, exercise, diet, medical care, and sometimes therapy or guidance to help assure our own integrity.

Where Is the Resurrection in Physical Decline?

Often it is agonizing to watch when vital people slowly, gradually deteriorate. If you spend enough time in hospitals, you develop the ability to intuit which shoe will fall next—in terms of the next set of problems. One wonders, looking at increasingly fragile people: Lord, where is the new life here? Perhaps it is Pierre Teilhard de Chardin who offers us a gleam of meaning and hope.

THE PURPLE RAINBOW

Teilhard wrote of aging, growth, evolution, and the mystery of the resurrection as a process of Christogenesis. Christogenesis is the process of moving toward greater oneness and congruence with the Risen Christ. The Risen Christ was not a resuscitated Christ. No, the Risen Christ had a continuity with the historical person Jesus, but He was nonetheless different. He was glorified, transformed. Jesus took on a glorified, physical presence, but He was and is essentially Spirit. In part, the victory of the Resurrection is the victory of the gradual Spiritualization of mere physical matter.

It comforts me to view the aging of the people that I love, indeed my own aging, as a gradual process of liberation, redemption, glorification, the spiritualization of physical matter, leading to Christogenesis, which is also Pneuma-genesis—oneness in the Holy Spirit with God the creator—Parent and the glorified Christ.

I pray through these thoughts, when on vacations or other overnights. I now tuck in the two people who used to tuck me in, and I check on them during the night as they once checked on me. They who were once giants in my perception now appear small in their beds.

CHAPTER SIX

When Celibates Fall In Love

My graduate work in psychology was done at the Alfred Adler Institute in Chicago. Adler and his disciple Rudolph Dreikers advocated a concept called "social interest." Social interest refers to the drive in human beings to relate, to communicate, to be one with others. At the heart of social interest is a recognition of the essential equality of all human beings. The Adlerian school feels that neurosis is found in the perceived need to be either inferior to or superior to others. Mental health, it says, is the wanting to be equal with—neither below nor above. The craving for "special-ness," is a form of emotional dysfunctioning. Specialness frustrates relationships.

The Adlerian lens has certainly made me re-interpret how the Catholic Church—at least in the past—formed priests. The very word "seminary," speaking of a type of hothouse where "vocational seeds" are planted and grown, connotes a setting apart, a specialness. The jargon that we hear from hierarchical circles of "the ontological difference between priest and laity because of the sacrament of Holy Orders" perpetuates the specialness myth. I fear that the specialness theme is still part of seminary education, as the priesthood as we have known it engages in a kind of death dance before inevitable transformation. The question I have been wrestling with regarding priestly formation is: Have we trained both men and congregations for an "ontologically special priesthood?" If declared ontologically special, are priests not hopelessly frustrated in attempting to relate to laity, who are only ordinary? Are not ordinary people frustrated in trying to understand someone who is ontologically special?

Do seminaries sometimes mass-produce neurosis or muted sociopathy?

The Breakdown of the Myth

I remember many of us, before ordination in the early seventies, wrestling personally and with others, with the decision for celibacy. I fear often the wrestling, while using emotive language, was more intellectual than emotional in the "hothouse." Celibacy became more of a real struggle for us when we moved into full-time ministry in the day to day life of neighborhood parishes and families.

My struggle with celibacy—intellectual then and emotional now—is that I believe it to be a charism, that is, a gift of the Spirit. We really ought not to legislate about charisms. For all who accept ordination to claim that they have the charism of celibacy is simply a ritualized fallacy. It cannot be true. For many, then, celibacy is part of the package if you feel called to the life of priestly leadership in the Roman Catholic Church. Note: I am not saying all priests should marry, for that calling also is a gift. There ought, I believe, to be married priests and celibate priests, male priests and female priests. And there ought to be much more true struggling with discernment concerning one's charisms and true vocational direction.

Not enough Catholics realize that, though there were attempts to legalize celibacy as far back as the fourth century, it was not universally imposed until the twelfth century as a requirement for priests in the Western rite. Similarly, few of us were taught about the powerful role of women in the New Testament and early Christian centuries, wherein widows and deaconesses exercised authority often equal to that of the priest.

The Breakdown of the Myth: Father Mike

The story of Mike is legion. He is a good priest, with a love of people and a deep spirituality. He bounded into his priesthood after ordination with much enthusiasm. Lonely? It was a word he did not worry about much—except on days off when his buddies from the seminary could not spend time with him or on vacations if the same group had to arrive later in the trip or leave early. In those alone moments, an overwhelming sense of sadness and fear would come over Mike. He would quickly bury it by creating activity for himself. He above all did not want to deal with it. It was frightening. It hurt. It was profound loneliness.

Though intellectually gifted and somewhat emotionally stable, Mike shares with many priests a great problem: difficulties in forming intimate relationships—with either men or women. If you are trained to be special, it is difficult to share your humanity and vulnerability with another human being. There were a number of women Mike had worked closely with in parish projects over the years. Some he had found attractive, but he had always effectively erected walls that distanced him from doing more than noticing their attractiveness. Except in one case. Mike had begun an adult education program with the assistance of a young woman in her mid-twenties. Mike was in his mid-thirties, now—with a little less enthusiasm; a little more jaded, having experienced the trauma which transfers from one parish to another can create. He noticed something about himself, in this his third parish: he was much less interested in getting personally involved in the lives of people in the parish. He had done that hundreds of times in the first two assignments. By and large the relationships did not endure, and so Mike grew cynical about something he was not too good at anyway—relationships.

But there was this one person, this young woman, Kathleen, the person working with Mike on adult education. He noticed himself enjoying that ministry most of all—because he did it with Kathleen. In fact, he would frequently create needs that called for extra one-on-one meetings with her. He found himself thinking about her a great deal in his free time, wondering when next she might stop in the rectory. When she did stop in, his day changed. The drudgery of program planning, counselling, teaching religion in school, lifted when she appeared. She was like a ray of sunshine in his life.

Kathleen was a single woman, so Mike became pre-occupied with her safety. Frequently he would see her home to her apartment and stay awhile for a drink. Those "in the know" around the rectory began to notice that Mike and Kathleen were becoming more than the leaders of parish adult education. When rumors began to fly about Kathleen and Mike, Kathleen was most upset. She did not want to be labeled "the priest's girl friend." Mike took more of a "let them be damned" attitude toward the gossips. He was becoming less and less discreet about his feelings for Kathleen. Mike gradually realized that for the first time in his life he had fallen in love. When Kathleen dated other men, this became a source, not so much of jealousy, but great pain for Mike.

He did not know Kathleen's sexual history or her current activity. All he knew was that his passion for her was increasing. The thought of not being with her intimately, as someone may have already been, or might be in the present, caused his heart to ache. One day, after a meeting in the office, Kathleen rose to leave. Mike stopped her, embraced her, and then initiated a passionate kiss. Both willingly surrendered to the experience. They stepped back from each other and stared in each other's eyes. Without speaking, they acknowledged the truth: they were in love. The office door was closed. No one outside Mike's office knew what had happened. Mike and Kathleen knew, however.

THE PURPLE RAINBOW

There were more experiences of private embracing and kissing—some more intense than the initial one. Mike would have bouts of guilt about these experiences, but then a rational side would kick in. He would say to himself that he was entitled to such moments of tenderness. He had been deprived of them, because of celibacy, all his life.

Time alone with each other, drinks, dinner—they increased. Through it all Kathleen's anxiety increased. Where was this relationship going? What was it about this Church that would not permit two people who love each other to be with each other? Why did she have to feel like a sinner? Why did the relationship have to be a secret? Why could Kathleen and Mike not possibly proclaim to the world that they had discovered something beautiful with each other?

Mike's cynicism with the Church grew. There were days when he was sure that he should leave the priesthood and marry Kathleen. In his mind he created scenarios about the future. He would become an instructor at a graduate school for pastoral ministry. He would become a full-time counselor. He went so far as to talk to leaders of other denominations, feeling he would always, somehow, be involved in the work of ministry. If his own Church would not have him, he would go where he was wanted. Though some of the interviews were appealing, especially the one with the Episcopalian rector which showed the great similarities between the Roman and Anglican traditions, the thought of leaving the Church frightened him. Being Catholic was as much a part of the fiber of his being as being an Irish American.

Patrick J. Brennan

What had begun innocently, if not naively, was now torturous for both Mike and Kathleen. They obviously wanted intercourse, but both had decided the act was meant for a committed, marital relationship. In addition, neither wanted to live a double life—a public persona in conflict with the private lives they were living behind closed doors at her apartment.

There were other pressures, one of which was his family. Mike came from a large, traditional, Irish family. What would brothers, sisters, mother, father, and extended family do if they learned of his leaving the priesthood to marry? He knew! He would be disowned. He would have Kathleen, yes. But he would have no other family. His soul and mind ravaged with conflict, Mike sought the help of a psychotherapist.

The therapist tried to bring rationality to Mike's situation, which was extremely emotional.

"Mike," he would say. "You cannot have both. Maybe your love is good and moral, but you are trapped in time and history. You cannot be a married priest."

"Then what do I do?" Mike would tearfully plead.

"My advice," said the therapist, "is to make a clean break with Kathleen. Both of you go cold turkey. Stop seeing each other. And she will have to drop all involvement in parish programs with you."

Mike did not like what he heard. He began to skip therapy sessions, because he knew he would not or could not follow the therapist's advice. It was not that easy. He could not just pretend that Kathleen had died. He could not treat her like waste to be discarded. Perhaps he had to control the relationship more and better, but he could never deny how much he loved her.

There were to be many more days on the cross for Kathleen and Mike. Kathleen's cross, like that of so many women who become involved with priests, was quiet, stifled—suffered alone. She continually had to change the emotional gears of her mind and heart to relate to Mike's new "friends forever, but no marital commitment" thrust. I am more aware of Mike's cross. The inevitable happened. To protect herself and prepare for her future, Kathleen began to date other men. With several, she became quite close, quite intimate. Part of Mike rejoiced with her and for her. But a larger part was devastated as he noticed the little touches and glances of intimacy which passed between Kathleen and her latest boyfriend or later her fiance.

Weddings became particularly difficult for Mike to perform. The sights and sounds of the wedding ceremony were like daggers cutting into his heart. Often, unnoticed, tears would form in his eyes as he witnessed the marriage of a couple that he sensed especially loved each other. Mike's stand toward Kathleen over the years became one of sacrificial love: whatever he could do to help her, befriend her, make life easier for her, he did—always from the side, especially as others entered her life. As Mike tried to be true to himself, practice integrity, he had to admit two profound truths—he felt called to be a priest, and he loved Kathleen. Those two realities would always have to fit in his heart, even if the institutional Church said they were incompatible.

Patrick J. Brennan

Kathleen married recently—a successful lawyer with whom she seems quite happy. She never actually asked Mike to officiate at the wedding. When she announced her wedding plans to Mike, he felt a sudden stab of pain in his stomach. He abruptly announced: "Oh, I am already committed to a speaking engagement in Ireland at that time." End of conversation.

The day Kathleen was married, Mike searched through the cemeteries of County Kilkenny, with much inner turmoil, looking at grown-over headstones, seeking out his roots.

Mike confesses that he would not trade the experience of loving Kathleen for any experience he had had in life. The hurt of her loss he would carry in his heart forever. The children that Kathleen and he will never have are emotional stillbirths that he still grieves. But loving her taught him much about the nature of true sacrificial love. In a clerical culture that often sublimates sexual needs and desires in vacations, alcohol, or food, he had found someone that he loved, without any hope of return.

He still goes back and forth in his mind: Why did he stay a priest? Is it a true vocational calling, or was he simply afraid to make a life change? Was the therapist right: He was better made for a celibate priesthood than for married life? He has leanings as to what the answers to those questions are, but he does not know with certainty.

He only knows this: It was much better to have loved and lost than never to have loved at all.

CHAPTER SEVEN

Why Is God Taking Away My House?
Losing Home

"Stop and put up your hands!" The plain clothes policeman and FBI agents meant what they ordered. They would have shot if my friend and I had not stopped in our tracks. We were "innocent criminals." As college students, home for the summer, my friend and I were simply intrigued by the late 60s black demonstrations on the southwest side of Chicago in Marquette Park, and also on the northwest side—still in the city, but close to O'Hare field. We were simply taking a shortcut through the alleys of a neighborhood still known as Wrightwood-Ashburn, in Chicago, a southwest community that is adjacent to the now infamous Marquette Park area. Young Jesse Jackson, in the late 1960s, had orchestrated a march down 79th Street, the main artery, through the neighborhood of our family home.

You have to grow up on the southwest side of Chicago to understand the racism that is still alive and active there. My friend and I were only collegiate curiosity seekers. But the racial tension present twenty years ago in that community was explosive. In fact, it still is. We had been stopped by law officers concerned about Ku Klux Klan threats against Martin Luther King, Jr. and Jesse Jackson.

Now, twenty years later, police have had to give special protection to the block that I grew up on—in response to one black woman whose home was fire bombed and another black couple whose garage had been spray painted with the message, "Get out, nigger!"

It has been my hope these past few years that the neighborhood that I grew up in would become a "new Beverly"—a replica of a southwest side community that has worked diligently at equitable integration and neighborhood stabilization. This was not to be the course of my family's neighborhood. Two black families seemed acceptable to the many on the block. But then, more and more whites sold and only blacks would buy in the area.

The block meetings increased. "There's no need to move," the community organizer and I protested at block meetings. Here is an opportunity to stem "whites running." Most of the whites in the gatherings agreed, but their agreement was truly notional. To have blacks in the hitherto all-white area was clearly an affront to social expectations and customs.

One by one, our block has emptied of white families and couples. Some the most militant who would "never move" have become "block busters." In the course of the last summer, the neighborhood has changed to almost 50% black. Who is refusing to flee? Older white couples and widows, largely senior citizens.

THE PURPLE RAINBOW

My family is among those who have not "run." Oh, we could, but my family has a growing sense of the rights of the black community. To a degree this has prompted us to keep our home, while others have moved. But our emotions have also kept us there. The home is a shrine to so many memories—my parents' marriage, my brother's and my growing up.

I noticed an initial reluctance to move in both my mother and father despite their faltering health. Though not racially liberal early on in life, they have grown to appreciate their new black neighbors. In turn, the recently arrived black families have tended well to my parents' needs.

The neighborhood transition has accelerated. Friends of close to forty years are coming over to say good-bye. The multiple good-byes are heart wrenching. What we, as Irish Catholics, are experiencing is a total, cultural shift. What blacks have experienced for centuries, we are now experiencing: We are the minority now. When I walk from my car to the house during the summer, I hear the urban rock of the boom blasters. I rather humbly walk into my home of close to forty years. As an Irish American, I now am a minority in an African-American community. I am being sensitized to the feelings that blacks have had all these years in the United States.

Confronting Racism

What has amazed me throughout this neighborhood transition is the wisdom and durability of its senior citizens. People who could have functioned as pillars of the neighborhood, effecting racial balance and harmony, have irrationally fled. It has not mattered that the new entrants are middle class, with sound jobs and values similar to the white families who have been living there. The future of the community, the young adults and middle age couples, left simply because the new neighbors are black. The black families pleaded for them to stay. It is true: Chicago is the nation's most racially divided city. The prophets throughout the process have been the senior citizens. Not just their physical disabilities or their fixed incomes, but their dedication to the neighborhood and their openness to their new black neighbors have kept them in their homes. It is the seniors especially who have knocked down the walls of racism by getting to know and become friends with the new arrivals.

Early in the process of the neighborhood change, reflecting on chronic illnesses as well as major demographic shifts around her, my mother would ask me, "Why is God taking away my house, too?" My mother and father have learned God is not taking away their home. Rather, all is in flux—our bodies, our minds — even our neighborhoods go through stages. As the neighborhood welcomed Irish, Poles, Germans, and Italians —now it needs to assimilate Hispanics, African-Americans, Asians, Arabians, and Persians. The miracle I am experiencing is white senior citizens, in the past racist by their own admission, getting beyond skin color and dialect to get to know previously perceived enemies as people—not a great deal unlike themselves.

THE PURPLE RAINBOW

You Can't Sell A Shrine

I mentioned earlier that the house almost seems like a shrine, a sacred place. My mother weeps when she declares that she wants to die in that house, to stay there until God calls her. It is a small, five-room ranch house. Not much to look at! Some cars today cost more than the original price of the house. What is more of a problem concerning the house than racial change is the now fragile health of the two proprietors. The mid-life sons and daughter of these senior citizens try to be helpful, but they cannot do everything. I notice now weeds that would not have been there a few years ago, when my mother and father were on top of things. Snow and ice removal during winter is a constant concern. Living far from them and commuting in to tend to them a few times a week can be draining. The practicality and efficiency of moving them to a condo with no maintenance worries and close to my brother or to me often seems attractive. But I have emotional blockage toward selling the house.

I was discussing this recently with a woman, a friend of mine. She poetically summed up the dilemma. She was the first to name the house "a shrine." "It is a shrine to your mother's motherhood, your father's fatherhood, their marriage, the growth of their two sons. You don't sell a shrine—not easily."

Memories

I walk inside and outside of the house—with a sense of nostalgia now. I walk from room to room and have memories. I remember a little 12-inch Motorola TV in the early 50s that brought into our living room "I Love Lucy," "Make Room for Daddy," Jack Benny, Milton Berle, Jackie Gleason, John Cameron Swayze, "The Kraft Music Hall," Perry Como, "Studio One," "The U.S. Steel Hour," and Howdy Doody. I remember sick days off from school, lying on the couch. I remember being taken from that couch to a hospital for oxygen because of my childhood asthma. I remember a little Victrola record player that played only 45s—boring stuff my father liked—Vaughn Monroe, Lawrence Welk, Wayne King. I remember the 1960 addition of a family room on the back of the house, and how the living room became something special—for company. The family room became the new gathering place to talk, watch TV, read.

I walk through the bedroom that my brother and I shared and remember the times we had at play in that room. I look in the closet, where as a boy I operated a once-a-week Remco radio station that broadcast my programs for my mother who would only be in the kitchen. I look at their bedroom, a sacred place which we were not allowed in too much. I walk through the basement, and remember roller skating down there, the train set we had, scaling water pipes that once seemed like huge oak trees. I remember four dogs—Bingo I, Chipper, Bingo II, and Bingo III.

What Is At Stake?

I desperately want to protect my parents from the hurt of losing their home. I could find them an apartment, a condo, a townhouse with great immediacy. But immediacy and efficiency are not the most important values at stake. It is, rather, maintaining a spirit of openness for new neighbors and a sense of continuity for older people who resist change.

The real bottom line is that "the shrine" cannot be held by us forever. My mother and father have serious health problems. Maintaining a home for them is becoming quite difficult: grass, snow, weeds. One of them most likely will pass on before the other. The more the neighborhood changes, and there is re-segregation, the greater chance there is of gangs, drugs, crime, and violence entering the neighborhood. While their immediate plans are to stay, the inevitability of our family not being in that house is not far off. I fear that inevitable day, what it will do—either to them or to me.

My Home

I am getting in touch with the depth of the bottom line. In fact, my greatest fear is personal. That little five-room house on the southwest side of Chicago is, in effect, the dominant home that I have known for thirty-eight years. I have wondered whether my own reluctance to let go of "the shrine" was a function of being a celibate. While that might be a factor, conversations with other people have convinced me that the loss of one's childhood home is traumatic for many people.

A forty-year-old married woman with children told me recently how she fears the inevitable sale of the home that her parents still live in. It is, for her, a kind of foundational symbol. A senior citizen recently told me that the only home she ever dreams of is her childhood home. Perhaps this is different for children of the present age who have had to adapt to the middle class nomadic style. More than when I was a child, children today have to accept multiple geographical moves—based on their parents' careers.

Allan Bloom in *The Closing of the American Mind*, a reflection on American culture and education, laments this situation. He comments that families have become completely tied up with what they do and what they have. You must *move* in this mileau, to wherever what you do will continue to contribute to what you can have. Pragmatics now dominate family life. Family life is eroding. Family erosion, Bloom believes, has contributed also to "spiritual bleeding," or the failure of families to pass on spiritual values, traditions, and rituals.

I was a child of a different culture, a unique ethnicity, a set of values different from those of popular wisdom today. I have come to realize that I am the one having the greatest emotional difficulty with the inevitability of selling the shrine. My problem is two-fold. First, I have a tendency to try to control everything for the good of my parents. The screen of my imagination is filled with all sorts of configurations of possibilities concerning the future, what to do with them or him or her, what to do with *it*—the house. Secondly, I have a deep craving for a *home*, a place of stability, stillness, comfort, warmth, love, a place of acceptance and unconditional love, a place where I feel rootedness.

THE PURPLE RAINBOW

Surrendering Control; Finding a New Home

I have come to realize that when I find myself obsessed about what to do with the house, I am trying to control the future too much. At such moments of awareness, I try to practice prayerfully surrendering the people, the things, the house, to God the Creator-Parent. I largely do this with an equally obsessive-compulsive, mantra-like prayer style, in which I repeatedly turn over my worries to God. The words of the mantra-like prayers change, but the emotional tone that I practice is the same. I am always equivalently saying to God: "Lord God, my need to control is a self-deception. I am trying to convince myself of my own power. The truth is that I am powerless in the face of life's mysteries. I recognize my powerlessness. I surrender the house and all these worries to you, the source of true power. And, Lord, your power is love."

There remains the need for a home. I reflect on the words of Jesus that he, the Lord of life, did not have a place to lay his head. Jesus did not have his own physical home. Yet he was most often "at home" in the world. The experience of "at homeness," inner peace, "at oneness" that pervaded Jesus' inner life seems to have come from a profound feeling of bondedness to Abba, his experience of the Creator-Parent. The "at homeness" seems to have been rooted also in his profound reverence for life, especially his fellow human beings. Jesus was neither competing with nor less than; he sought only to be one with brothers and sisters. With home in his heart, Jesus could move from town to town, place to place and still feel rooted. In this age of seeking out "our roots," perhaps the roots that Jesus found are ones we all ought to seek out—a rootedness in God through the Holy Spirit.

So—a rather mundane issue, what to do with an aging home—is teaching me much about my own neurotic need to control and the antithesis to that, faithful surrender to God. The process is teaching me to seek a home within myself that is rooted in love of God and others.

Racism as a Prison

Driving through the areas where the urban poor dwell, I often get the feeling that people living in run down buildings and projects are almost as if they are in jail —confined within the cell of urban blight and poverty. The experience of neighborhood change has convinced me that those who run, take flight, are in their own kind of prison. The building blocks of the prison are prejudice, fear, and ignorance. What a richness there would be in more of our urban areas if we could experience a healthy mixture of white, ethnic, black, Hispanic, Asian, Jewish, Protestant, and Catholic. To the degree we still cannot accomplish this integration, we as racial/ethnic groups and religious sects are locking ourselves in our own prisons. We are missing what Jesus intended, wanted when he preached and worked for the Reign of God. Are urban blacks locked in prisons of projects? Of course! But so are the upper middle class and the upper class in their fine condos, townhomes, and houses. They are in a different kind of prison—one resisting the enrichment of other cultures and traditions.

The Neighborhood As Paschal Mystery

In a changing neighborhood, the paschal mystery is present and alive. The paschal mystery is present in both individuals and the community collectively. For individuals—some pulling up stakes and leaving, others struggling to stay—there is the pain of transition and goodbyes. Hopefully these death moments, approached with faith and prayer, will lead to new life, new beginnings for the newcomers to the area, for those who choose to stay, and for those who move to another environment. For the neighborhood, there is the possibility of resurrection to an integrated neighborhood—approximating the equality and justice of the Kingdom of God. There is also the collective possibility of the community disintegrating into a re-segregated ghetto that becomes problematic and impoverished. For individuals, for a neighborhood, the paschal mystery, passage is at work—hopefully life through death to new life. As with all cases of spiritual passage, the process can be short-circuited and get locked into a posture of death.

For individuals, for the community, there is the inevitability of pain in this passage. At a recent meeting of a divorce support group, a gentleman described the situation of his recent uncoupling with his wife as one of "being in between." He knows something new and different will emerge as a life pattern. But all he can do now is face and embrace the dis-ease, the discomfort of being "in between." In the facing and embracing, he is trying to trust that the passage of "in-betweenness" will be transformed into new life for him. Right now, however, it hurts. His words struck me. I, we, need to practice greater trust in periods of in-betweenness like neighborhood change. We ought not to reach for quick solutions.

A gerontologist recently told me about her own family. Some years ago, her mother and father were living in a changing neighborhood. They also were advancing in age and seemed to their middle-aged children unable to tend to and care for their home. They had been in the home for forty years. Her brothers decided for the parents that they should be moved to safety and greater ease in a suburban condo. After the move, the mother lived one month. Her dad, left as a widower, died four months later. Deciding for older people, she warned me, or in my words, trying to avoid the passage, the in-between times pain of neighborhood change—could actually cause greater harm than help. Her well-meaning brothers actually expedited the death of their parents by pulling them from their roots. True the roots were changing, were in passage. But perhaps there was something new and better waiting for them in that re-configured neighborhood. She, then he, died of apparently broken hearts.

On Becoming Adult and Leaving Home

A priest friend of mine recently told me that he returned to his neighborhood of origin—now in a totally re-segregated area of Chicago. He was at a parish anniversary celebration. Afterward, he drove to his old house in the neighborhood. To his surprise, it was unoccupied and boarded up. Risking being caught as a trespasser, yet still feeling some ownership over the building, he pulled out already loose boards and entered the house via a window close to the steps of the old bungalow. He walked through his old home. It was a dreadful experience. Where there had been love, parties, companionship, there was decay, dirt, and abandonment. He had a strange feeling that this was not his home any longer. Indeed it was not. He had already begun the process of finding home within himself. Finding "home within oneself" does not just mean being at peace with self and God, as I previously described it. It means also that the people that were or are home for you, you will carry in your heart with you forever. We all carry within us hurts and unresolved problems with our family members, but most of us carry also precious memories and moments. It is these inner experiences of parents, brothers, and sisters that my friend treasures now, not the false security of a physical building.

If and when I make the final tour of a very special building, before I close the door for the last time, I plan to take more than boxes of things with me. I will store in my heart also precious memories and people—always alive in the Spirit. I will leave that physical thing that I call the old family home, but I will have the best of home in my heart. Maybe, then, I will begin to glimpse the freedom of Jesus, who had no place to lay his head, but always was at home. Maybe I will begin to taste the fullness of being adult.

CHAPTER EIGHT

The Loss of a Child

I never quite understood Aunt Ag. My mother's sister, she was a crusty, abrasive woman—yet kind. She had played nurse to my brother and me as infants as well as to my cousins. Underneath the hardness, the abrasiveness, was love and kindness that she showed largely to children. Maybe in the eyes of the children she bathed and cleaned, she saw a glimmer of the eyes of her son, Ronnie. Ronnie died in 1942, five years before I was born. I never knew him, but as with all dead brothers, sisters, or cousins, Ronnie became somebody for me. I often wondered about him, imagining what he was like.

Ronnie, they say, was a strong, handsome little boy, until about age three. Then he began to show signs of abdominal swelling and other parts of his body became puffy as well. My maternal grandmother expressed concern, which led Ag and Johnny, her husband, to take the child to a doctor. The rather primitive testing of the time revealed acute kidney disease. Ag and Johnny were told that Ronnie had only months to live. His dysfunctioning kidneys deteriorated further. The swelling grew. Soon he was so bloated he had trouble walking. Ag and Johnny had to move their little boy around in a wagon.

Ronnie died. Johnny and Ag went on to shower their affection on nieces and nephews. Then Ag lost Johnny to the same kidney ailment that had taken Ronnie. A woman who had lost her son was suddenly widowed. Then, later in life, Ag was diagnosed as having terminal cancer. It was quite advanced by the time of the diagnosis —in the lungs and liver. I remember being alone with Ag on a snowy, Sunday afternoon in November, right after she heard she was dying. I had never known a person who had lost everything: child, husband, health. She was indeed a female Job. I struggled with what to say. I held her hand and said, ''Ag, is there anything you want to talk about?'' She stared in my eyes with a look of recognition. She knew that I knew. For the first time I saw Ag weep. She cried deeply, as if she were crying not just for herself, but for Ronnie and Johnny also. After crying for awhile, she said, ''No, there's nothing I want to talk about.''

Ag was a strong-willed, faithful person. Through her multiple losses, she prayed, trusted, and then lived— ''get on with it,'' as she would often say. This was how she approached chemotherapy, too—with courage, conviction, and prayerfulness. It was pain that was to be endured for perhaps a greater good.

As she lay dying one morning, in a semi-coma, she sat straight up in bed, opened her eyes, and stared. The sudden movement was a stronger physical movement than she had previously seemed capable of. I have often wondered if perhaps in those final hours, she saw or sensed Ronnie, Johnny, and the Lord with her. As several of us talked her over to the other side of death, hoping her hearing was still good as we prayed with her, she truly resembled Christ on the cross. With her bald head, and frail body, on the cross of the bed, she had become truly Christified, one with Christ in suffering and death. Call it Irish determination or Christ-like faith, her approach to every loss was faith, prayer, and action—little time given to self-pity.

Good-Bye, Margie

I began to understand the depth of Ag and Johnny's pain in losing Ronnie, when I became a teenager. During my freshman year of high school, my young cousin, Margie, died at age nine. She had always been a frail child, but no one in the family thought she was close to death when she had her last bout of a viral infection. It turned out to be a type of encephalitis, an infection that found its way to her brain, resulting in a high, death-dealing fever.

It was September, 1961, a Friday. My second day of high school. I was the last one to leave the house, then the phone rang. My father informed me that my mother had been summoned from work to the hospital to support her sister and brother-in-law—Margie had died. I went to school that day, and sat in a kind of dense fog. The teachers, the other guys in class, were far from me. I was lost in the hallway traffic. I was fourteen, in a high school, commuter preparatory seminary. As an adoles-

92

cent, I was entering, via Margie's death, into the mystery of life.

How could a nine-year-old die? It is not supposed to work this way. Older people died. Nine. That's not far from fourteen. I could die. How must Charlie and Monica, my aunt and uncle feel? What should I say to them when I see them? Was I good enough, kind enough to her when she lived? How will I feel when I look at her, dead? Will I get sick? How will I act? I wondered as teachers and other teens were busy about school.

In fact, when I saw her I cried. I did not know what to say to Monica and Charlie. The wake was held in the home—perhaps this was one of the last times this was done in the Chicago area. Throughout the hot, pre-air conditioning September wake and funeral both parents had an obvious grief, but perhaps more a shock and a hollowness that seemed untouchable and unreachable. This deep, heavy hollowness persisted for days, months, and years. In fact, the twenty-seventh anniversary of Margie's death just passed. My family sent, as we usually did, a commemorative card. Monica called with gratitude and remarked that not too many mark Margie's passing anymore. Her voice communicated that even twenty-seven years later, the loss of her child was still a painful wound.

The unfolding lives of Monica and Charlie have taught me that the death of a child, your child, is a wound from which parents never recover. The pain only becomes a bit muted with the passing of time. They also have helped to teach me that God is not the cause of our problems but rather the source of healing for our pain.

Patrick J. Brennan

At the time of Margie's death, I did not realize how lightening would strike again, even closer to home.

Justin

I have taken personality tests that place me high on the scale of intuition. I sense things, hunch things, perceive things—often before they become apparent to others. For weeks I had felt uncomfortable with my sister-in-law's second pregnancy. I did not know why. I communicated my fears to a young woman in my office, and she told me to hush up and not say such things.

One fall morning in 1982, I awoke at 3:30 am with a stir. I had a sense of something being wrong. I sat up in bed with my heart pounding. And then the phone rang. It was my brother. His voice was cracking. "Will you come to the hospital right away? Kathy had a son, but . . . but . . . there's something wrong with the kid's heart. They . . . they don't know if he's going to make it."

I shook with cold and fear as I drove to Christ Hospital, in a southwest suburb of Chicago. As I drove, I did not know what to pray for. Part of me told God if the child was badly damaged, it would be a burden too great for the two of them to carry. It would be better if the child died quickly. Part of me prayed that the damage would be only slight, reversible, and that they would take home a healthy son.

I went first to the nursery, and asked to see my nephew. They showed me a little red haired infant in an incubator. I was greatly alarmed at what I saw. There was obviously more than heart damage afflicting this child. His appearance betrayed multiple cerebral and physical defects. To breathe, he needed the constant assistance of a respirator. My heart sank. This was a very sick little boy. I asked the nurse about his condition. "Very bad," she said. "These rarely make it; they go in a few days. If they live, it is never more than for two years, and they require oxygen and special feeding because of distorted intestinal organs." "Oh, I see!" I swallowed. "I better go to see my brother and sister-in-law."

I found them together; he was standing over her bed, holding her hand. Their eyes were red from already shed tears. My brother struggled to be optimistic. "We don't know how this will go. He may survive. They may be able to do surgery. We'll take him home and see what happens." I held my silence.

"How did he look to you, Pat?" asked Kathy. "Not bad," I lied. My brother asked me to baptize the baby "Justin William" and I did. Afterward, we stood in the hall and talked. An aide came up after the baptism and asked which of us was William, the father. My brother identified himself. "Here's your son's baptismal certificate," said the unknowing aide. "And congratulations on your son, Mr. Brennan!" The crushing paradox of her words exploded inside my brother. He ran to the nearest stairwell to hide his sobbing. I ran after him. For the first time in my life, I held him as he cried. He stepped back, and looked at me. "Why is this happening to me?" he asked. "All I've ever wanted was a son. How can this happen?" I stared back at him. "I don't know," I said almost defiantly. I who studied philosophy, theology, and psychology—the Catholic answer man—I had no easy, pious answers for this profound question. "I don't know why good people suffer." I simply continued to hold him.

Telling Grandparents

How do you tell elderly people, who are not well, that their hoped and prayed for grandchild has multiple birth defects? I did not want to shock them, cause a heart attack or stroke. I drove to my parents' house under the pretense of having left something there the last time I had visited. I needed it; so I would stop for breakfast.

Over coffee, I slowly began. "Ma, Pa, Kathy delivered." "Is it a boy or girl?" my mother asked. "It's a boy." "Oh, a little boy!" she marvelled. "Is everything OK?" "No, everything is not OK," I responded. "There are problems with the little boy's heart, and some other complications." My mother has great internal courage and faith. "Pat, is he bad?" "Yes, he is." "Then it would be better if God would take him than to have him suffer." My father agreed. Their acceptance and faith put me at ease. I thought I would have two hysterical people to handle. We joined hands and prayed for the little boy, Justin, and for his mom, and his dad.

By evening, Kathy's family were tending to her. So I took my brother to his home to spend the night with him. He fell asleep as soon as he sat down to watch the 10 o'clock news. I eventually woke him up and escorted him up to bed, which he fell into fully clothed. I pulled the blankets over him. I walked down the hall and looked into the new baby's room. The crib, the toys, the new wallpaper—all had been arranged in anticipation. I sat down on the stairs leading back down to the living room. I began to cry. I remember it being a different kind of crying—almost a groaning, a moaning, a cry of deep, deep sadness. Part of the tears were due to sitting on bombs all day, letting them go off inside of me, so that the hurt and alarm to others would not be too great. Now, alone, I had to deal with what those bombs had done to me.

The Phone Call

Early the next morning, the phone rang. I answered it. It was the hospital. Justin had taken a turn for the worse. It would be good if we could get there soon. I woke my brother. As I drove, he sobbed into a handkerchief. We both knew what was waiting for us.

Justin was already dead when we arrived. The staff told us to go and tell Kathy and console her. We did. She took it calmly; she had expected it. Then, a nurse came and invited us to look at the child, to say good-bye. They had him bundled up as if he were going home. All that showed was his face. The deformities and abnormalities were hidden now. He looked like a beautiful little baby sleeping. We stood in silence, and touched his little body. The nurse said, "Why don't you hold him?" Because he had always been cared for in an incubator, we had never held him. I was afraid. I felt overpowered, as if I might faint. "I can't," I thought, "but I'm here for them." My brother picked the child up, rocked him a little, bent down and kissed him on the forehead. I did the same. My sister-in-law did the same. We prayed and spoke to Justin, in the Spirit, briefly. Then, we filed out in silence, back to her room. We had shared a painful but comforting moment. Not only did Justin look like he was going home, we knew that he had gone home, that he was with the Father and Jesus in the Holy Spirit.

After Justin's death, my brother and I went to the funeral home. Joe Quinlan, a friend of mine, agreed to handle all the details. It became my chore to buy cemetery lots—something my family had yet to do. It is a rather sobering reality to buy burial ground for your nephew, your parents, your brother and sister-in-law—and yourself. Of course the family got a discount rate because of me. Yet I received the lousiest spot—at the foot of everyone else.

A priest friend and I celebrated the Eucharist for the immediate families in a chapel in the cemetery. The mood was subdued; most of the tears of shock, surprise, and loss had already flowed. We left the cemetery to begin the work of putting away baby things that would never be used and for Justin's parents to re-configure their marriage in the face of a major disappointment.

Having a Brother Who Died

Even in death, siblings influence each other. The dead brother or sister becomes mythic in a surviving child's mind, prompting much wondering. If negative comparisons are made (that is, that the living child is not measuring up to the potential exemplified by the deceased), the living child can in fact feel resentful toward the dead

THE PURPLE RAINBOW

brother or sister. My niece Heather spontaneously brings up Justin now, though she never saw him, and Justin never really lived long enough to inspire many stories. She once was staring at the Infant Jesus of Prague statue about a year ago (age six) and said, "That must be what my little brother looks like in heaven." At age six, both her religious imagination and her own preconscious wondering about her brother are at work. At other times, she sounds cheated that she is now an only child, and does not have a brother or sister to play with. Justin is a definite influence on the sister he never knew.

Now the Communion of Saints

I prayerfully speak to Justin everyday, asking him to pray for us, for me. An image from the "old Church" that is still important to me is the communion of saints. I encourage people who have lost someone through death to continue to speak to and communicate with their deceased loved one, to share their feelings of love, loss, guilt, and anger. We either believe in eternal life or we do not. If we do, we ought to act as if we do, pray as if we do. I know of one young woman who lost a grandmother who was important to her. When she began to acknowledge that her grandmother was still spiritually alive and to commune with her, she moved through powerful steps of emotional catharsis toward acceptance. Marie, a mother who lost her thirteen-year-old son, who was hit by a van while riding his bike, has regularly for the past twelve years prayed for her son, but also has spoken to him. He would be twenty-five years old now.

Patrick J. Brennan

I have vivid memories of many parents who have lost a child and of children who have lost a brother or sister. I remember Bill, one of my best friends, dying at age nineteen of acute leukemia. I remember Mike, one of the first teens I ever worked with, choking on a piece of meat in the pre-Heimlich maneuver days, as his friends watched him suddenly fall from a drive-in stool. I remember Tim, a young adult, going to work early one morning when his car was hit from behind by someone drunk and on other drugs. I remember going to the home with his parents to tell the rest of the family. I remember the anger, rage, hurt, grief, loneliness, and doubt I have felt at these times. Yet not even in the case of Justin, could I have known the parents' experiences.

A Response in Faith

Ronnie, Margie, Justin: our family did something quite spontaneously. We approached the losses in faith. The faith did not get rid of the pain. Rather it helped make sense of the pain and the pain simply became less intense as time passed. So the loss of a child brings with it a deep kind of pain. You never ''get over'' the loss; you always live in terms of it. My family's faith goes something like this: God did not cause those deaths. They happened. God is healing and help in the face of losing a child. He is healing to grieving parents and families. He is a reassuring Parent who holds the deceased child in His loving hands. Survivors and those who have passed on can rest in peace in God. It is important to keep in mind that grieving a child, indeed grieving anyone, is a process. It takes a lot of time. Frequently, changes in dream patterns (that is, starting to dream about a person after dreams have been blocked) are signs that the healing is coming. At times people can resist healing, hold on to grief, as a way of holding on to the child or other deceased person.

Though God does not cause these tragedies, I do believe he speaks powerfully through them. I feel everyone is "on purpose," meant to be here. Through our living and dying, the Spirit is speaking to others. In this perspective living and dying have deep meaning. Justin was, is a message, a spoken word, to us. As John Powell has written, for people of faith, there is a reason to live and a reason to die.

Mike and Rich

I would like to reflect briefly on how the death of a young person affects a minister, an outsider who is nonetheless involved with the family. I am conscious of two young people both of whom I taught or mentored as a deacon or a priest. I have briefly touched on both cases already.

Mike was in my first group in 1972. He was always around the rectory, in need of adult friendship and attention. He came from a dysfunctional home. When I left that parish, to go to another assignment, Mike continued to pursue me, with visits and phone calls. My new investment kept me from attending to Mike as much as I ordinarily would. One evening I received a phone call from my first assignment that Mike had suddenly died. It was not drugs, or suicide, or even a horrendous accident. He simply fell over while eating a hamburger with his friends at a drive-in. A piece of food got caught in his throat, blocking air.

I officiated at his wake and funeral. After the funeral, I had to drive a long distance to another state. I cried most of the way. My tears were tears of rage at the mysteries of life and death: what a senseless death—to choke on a hamburger. I cried tears of guilt, too, that often Mike had wanted more time from me. I had cheated him in the end; I had not heard fully his cries for help. I vowed in that car, that I would do all in my power to be a life-giver and helper for young people for the rest of my life. I certainly have not lived that vow perfectly. But Mike's death was a beginning for me of many dedicated years in youth ministry. In the mystery of Michael's death, resurrection had begun.

Rich was hit by a van on a Saturday afternoon. Without life support, he could not breath on his own from the moment of the accident. Brain damage was so severe he could not recover. I learned much from his parents, Marie and Dick, as I kept a five-day vigil at the hospital. I learned about faith and hope. They would pull no plugs. Perhaps God would work a miracle. I learned a greater sensitivity in the face of tragedy. Once when I spoke about her comatose son in the past tense, Marie gently reminded me that he was still alive. Finally, after he died and after his burial, I saw two parents who had lost so much of their lives, their only son, find new life and give new life to many Rich-like young people, as they dedicated the remaining years of their lives to the development of a youth center, a youth retreat program, and peer-to-peer ministries. They, who had been "inactive Catholics," became regular Church-goers. They never once blamed God, but found rather in God and community, hope and consolation. Rich's death, like Mike's, was mysteriously the beginning of new life for so many people.

I am reminded of Michelangelo's Pieta, the beautiful sculpture of Mary holding her dead son Jesus. It is a portrait of tragedy, an adult embracing her dead son. But in the tragedy, there is a poignant beauty. So it is with the loss of any child—obvious tragedy, but in the tragedy the beginning of a mysterious beauty and new life.

CHAPTER NINE

Sudden Departure

Tom was coming unravelled. He would call late at night and talk about how life was stacking the deck against him: love problems with his girlfriend, Lynn; job problems; financial problems. His conversations became increasingly distorted during the course of two weeks. Yes, he had life problems, but he saw them as a cosmic conspiracy against him. I know Tom at times relied on alcohol to occasionally blunt his pain, so I became increasingly worried. I asked Tom if he would see a counselor—not because he was sick, but just to learn better how to handle multiple stresses. He agreed.

Whatever took place between him and the counselor that I sent him to I don't know, but he came back with the idea that the therapist had declared him A-OK. The people with whom he was associating were the problem —that was his understanding of the counselor's insights. The midnight calls continued. I arranged for another interview with another counselor the following week.

THE PURPLE RAINBOW

There was an intensity in his calls now. He wanted problem people and problem situations fixed—now! I was in a particularly busy period myself—travelling and arranging programs for the Archdiocese of Chicago. I asked him to simply be patient—until the next week, when the new counselor would see him, his family, his girlfriend, whoever needed to be seen. He agreed on a Wednesday evening. He shot himself in the head Friday morning.

I never said good-bye.

Lynn never said good-bye.

It is hard to understand what was going on in Tom's mind to prompt him to a violent, self-destructive end. A friend of mine wrote me after the suicide, sensing my guilt about not having done anything to stop him. The friend's brother had committed suicide. Now, years after the trauma, she wrote:

> "I won't pretend that I can say anything that can remove the pain, but perhaps I can help you understand some of this better. Suicide never makes sense except to the person who does it, and also those of us who have been there. When my brother died, I kept saying that it would not have happened if he had not been drinking. Surely if he knew what he was doing, he would have chosen life. I no longer believe that.

> "The person considering suicide is unable to see any real value in his or her life. The key word is *real*. Another person could list all sorts of things that the person does that are of value. But for the person seriously considering suicide, each thing could be done by someone else just as well, if not better. There is the

105

feeling of 'What good am I to the world? A few people might cry at my funeral, but in a week or so, they'll forget I ever existed.' A suicidal person really believes those things.

"Suicidal people are filled with pain and anger. When I myself seriously considered suicide, I honestly believed that it was masochistic to go on living. I reached a point at which I believed a loving God would not want me to continue living with such awful pain. In some ways, a person who commits suicide has a greater trust in the love of God than the rest of us.

"Don't misunderstand me. I would never encourage anyone to commit suicide. But on the other hand, I cannot condemn those who do. I cannot believe that God will either.

"In one of your talks, you referred to one of Michelangelo's works, the Pieta, the sculpture of Mary holding her dead son, Jesus. You spoke of the work in terms of a 'tragedy that contained within itself a kind of beauty.' Think back to your own words, now, Pat. Although there is a lot of pain in this current tragedy, somewhere down the line someone will benefit from this suicide and see a beauty in the tragedy.

"As a result of my brother's suicide, I grew and was able to help people in ways that I never could otherwise. His death was not a *waste*, as people thought. Through the power of God and the mystery of things, his suicide resulted in good for many. Now I can see beauty in it.

"Hopefully, in the not too distant future, you and

all the people involved in this suicide will see 'beauty in the tragedy' that you are now experiencing.''

The faith in that letter sums up the main thrust of this entire book. Having survived her alcoholic brother's death, my female friend slumped to the point of considering taking her own life. The power of faith and supportive relationships somehow kept her going and prevented her from taking action on how she felt. The dominant image of new life coming from death, the dominant image of the paschal mystery, alive in her imagination, has helped her to re-interpret her brother's suicide. Though an objective evil and a tragedy, the power of God's grace has pulled good even from suicide. The Resurrection was and is victorious over death, suffering, and sin in all its forms.

Guilt

Those of us who are only a few weeks into grieving for Tom do not yet have the faith hindsight of the writer of that letter. Most of us are still at some stage of mourning, shock, guilt, or anger. Guilt is strong in me and in others. Could we have done more? Though he was a friend, and I do not do therapy with family or friends, could I have done more, intervened more strongly? I knew he was in pain. But in his frustration and struggle, he did not communicate the depth of pain that would lead him to shoot himself. Or maybe I just did not hear his cry for help.

But none of us heard it, if he was really communicating it: not his family, now his friends, not his girlfriend. She,

Lynn, is struggling in a special way. How could she be so close to a person for several years and not see or hear the depth of this man's struggle. Now she is wrestling with "what she did not do" to stop Tom from taking his own life.

Guilt after a suicide is one of the greatest sufferings people enter into, one of the crosses on which one must hang. It is easy for those not involved in the incident to speak objectively and rationally about how "Tom would have done it anyway." But for Lynn, Tom's family, and even the not-as-close, as I was and am, the horror of a young man taking his own life in his mid-twenties is escalating in the first weeks after the incident rather than lessening. The pain of guilt, of not having helped or helped enough, cannot be anesthetized. It must be experienced, felt. Perhaps only prayer, the support of others, and time will take the edge off of the guilt.

Missing Him

For Lynn, besides guilt, there is the cross of missing a man whom she loved. Though marriage was not in the immediate future, they had become extremely close friends. He was omnipresent in her life: morning coffee, late dinners, football games, weddings. All was taken from her with a gunshot. Now there are no phone messages, no flowers, no dinner partner. In many ways, Tom's difficulties have ended, and Lynn's have just begun—especially the guilt and loneliness.

The message I share with Lynn is not one that immediately satisfies her. When the "waves" (as she describes them) of guilt, or missing him, or the reality of the permanence of his physical loss seem to overcome her, she must, I tell her—

—stand her ground,
—name her feelings, with effort at precision,
—share those feelings with others and God,
—gain insight into them, specifically where they are coming from,
—cry, if need be, for a short period of time, but not languish in long periods of crying,
—"get on with it," that is "act as if" and immerse herself in others and meaningful activity, and
—pray for emotional healing.

Lynn will not engage in these therapeutic movements until and unless she has made a renewed decision for life. She has to say to herself and God and others, "I want to live. I had a life before Tom. I want to have a life after him." Without this motivation, Lynn, or anyone who has experienced a significant loss, will wander in darkness, meaninglessness, social isolation, and non-productivity.

I asked a consulting psychiatrist how long it would be before Lynn pulled together the pieces of her life. His answer surprised me. He said, "It depends on her. Recovery can take a short time or the rest of her life. She has all the resources she needs within her, the power of love and the power of God. A good part of her recovery depends on whether she wants to co-operate with those forces within her."

Patrick J. Brennan

A Network of Support

If you are a survivor of a suicide or similar loss, as Lynn, I cannot emphasize enough the importance of a support network. Lynn's lows or valleys are significantly leveled when people of faith and love, whom she respects, spend time with her, talk with her, and pray with her. The conversation need not even be about the tragedy. But people are so important for a grieving person. Without people, one climbs into a deep dark hole of isolation that maximizes the grief, guilt, and loneliness.

If you are a survivor, get off the dime and get the support. If you know a survivor, risk intruding to offer the support. In all cases choose life.

The Story of Carol: New Life from Death

I saw Carol, a young adult, several times, at the request of her parents. They were reluctant to allow her to go back to college because of the depression she was displaying. Carol obviously did not want to talk to me. Her one word answers gave evidence of her being there under pressure. At the end of the second session, I told Carol that I understood her not wanting to talk to me, that people have a right to choose their own helpers or guides. I simply asked that she find a priest or counselor at school if she continued to feel depressed and that she not deal with her problems with drugs, alcohol, or social isolation by herself.

Carol took her life the very first night at school. Alone, depressed, she obviously could not take the pain any longer. All of us who knew her were crushed in spirit. No one of us knew the depth of this young woman's pain. We missed all the signals, or she disguised them well. In this instance, family, friends, and priest went through months of guilt and also horror at the death of such a young person and the apparent senselessness of her death.

After hitting the very bottom of their grief, Carol's parents, two very faith-filled people, decided that they somehow wanted to draw life from this awful tragedy. Working with a priest trained in social work, they began a support group for the survivors of suicide. The success of the initial group has spawned other groups. Begun by Catholics, the notion of suicide survivors meeting for ongoing healing and support spread interdenominationally, ecumenically. Other denominations developed their own groups, or people of various faiths gathered in common groups.

Carol's death was indeed a tragedy, but I stand in awe at how faithful people and God's grace can turn even suicide into a source of life for others. Many people who also have lost a loved one through a self-destructive act have found hope and healing through the groups that began as a result of Carol's death. Part of faith is courage, courage for life, that comes from knowing that a God of love walks with us, even in the midst of pain and loss. Carol's family was able to tap that reservoir of faithful courage, to walk into their darkness, integrate the loss into themselves, then decide to co-operate with God's creative spirit in finding the new life already seminally begun in their daughter's death.

Patrick J. Brennan

Why Self-Destruction?

Boston journalist Donald Feder had a reflection on suicide in a column recently. He wrote that he felt at the root of the spate of suicides and self-destructive behaviors in America today is a spiritual malaise. Feder, and others, suggest that we have given birth to a generation of high achieving, spiritually apathetic young people, who do not know how to cope with or face struggle and failure. That reservoir of faithful courage that I referred to earlier simply is not there. Feder's advice is: in addition to counseling, therapy, etc., teach young people to pray, share with them a personal relationship with a loving God. This spiritual base is the grounding or foundation that many people in society today lack, and which leads them to escape pain through self-destruction. David Elkind, author of *The Hurried Child* and *All Grown Up and No Place to Go*, says that there is a whole generation of young people who have grown into adolescence and young adulthood without markers, that is, guides, mentors—adults who will help them find their place in the world. Key to finding one's place, Elkind has said in lectures and periodicals, is the discovery of a "companion God," with whom a young person can have a relationship of immediacy, spontaneity, and intimacy.

Without this encouraging God, people are left to death -dealing resources to handle pressure, stress, and disappointment. Perhaps this is why 80% of suicides involve drugs or alcohol abuse.

CHAPTER TEN

Compulsion

Michelle was like a lot of children who grew up with an alcoholic parent—she would never drink, at least never abuse alcohol, the way her mother had. Because of her drinking, Michelle's mother became plagued with a series of chronic health problems directly related to her drinking. Michelle operated on an attitude expressed in the title of Claudia Black's now classic book on adult children of alcoholics—*It Will Never Happen to Me.*

But Michelle did start drinking—during college, at parties. Unlike her peers, she knew just the right amount to drink to "get a buzz on," but not get knock-out, fall-down drunk. In her particular dorm, in her particular friendship group, partying was the way to do things. Drinking became *the* way to socialize. Drinking would go on late into the night and early in the morning. Stories were told the day after of "blowing lunch" and "worshipping the Lord of porcelain [the toilet]."

Graduation came. The old friendship group went its

113

many ways. Michelle got a job working with computers at a bank. The first time that she felt she might have a problem with alcohol centered on her job. Carrying school habits into life with her, Michelle regularly had a drink each day—either before dinner or as a nightcap before going to bed. She had to attend an overnight computer training session for her job. She got into her car and started on her way to the conference center. Suddenly, as she reported it to me later, she felt a stab of anxiety in her stomach. Would there be alcohol at this overnight? Would she be able to have a drink? Could she relax without a drink? Then—the thought came: Should I be so consumed with a craving for alcohol? Do I want it, need it too much? No, she answered herself: "It—alcohol dependency—will never happen to me."

Michelle's alcohol dependency did not become apparent to anyone but herself. Being an introvert by nature and conditioning, no one realized that she turned to alcohol in private moments, usually late at night, for rest and relaxation. Like many alcohol-abusers, Michelle exercised a great denial when it came to her alcohol use. She believed that she was in control, on top of things—even though frequently she felt awful on Mondays after weekend drinking bouts. Her job remained compulsively important to her, so she never allowed her drinking to seriously interfere with her performance on the job. But even that gave way eventually: her starting times after weekends became sporadic; the quality of her work performance was uneven at best.

The popular wisdom is that alcohol abusers have either a high or a low bottom. Michelle, a covert alcoholic, had a high bottom. Her bottoming out came in a series of rather undramatic events. One morning she found herself in the front seat of her car, lying across the seat, in a forest preserve close to her home. She remembered beginning the evening before with friends for dinner, and then there was a bar for some after dinner drinks, and—that is all she could remember. The forest preserve episode was Michelle's first major scare, a blackout. Her second series of events involved a number of small traffic accidents—none of which seemed tremendously significant in and of itself. There was a side-swiping of a post in a parking lot, the scraping of a downtown garage wall after a liquid lunch, and the near-miss head-on when she momentarily dozed on a rustic suburban road.

Intervention

Finally, a male friend cared enough to intervene to effect the high bottom. Bob, someone who dated Michelle off and on, noticed her one night at dinner. She was drinking more than eating. He simply mentioned it to her —"I'm getting concerned about how much you drink." She immediately grew defensive, arguing that her drinking was typical and within normal range. But as Bob looked deeply into her eyes, and she stared back, there was a moment of recognition. She remembered what one of her high school teachers had said many years before, quoting a Japanese proverb: "Man take first drink . . . Man take second drink . . . third drink take man . . ."

Was she taken? Did alcohol "have her?" She began to sob, as Bob looked on and took her hand. She began to talk. She explained her mother's alcohol dependency, her own college habits, and her own loneliness now. Several romances had fallen apart for her. Career remained important. She was making over $30,000 per year. But there was a part of her stranded, aching, isolated, and thirsty for love and companionship.

She had noticed, in her obsession over alcohol, that she ordered drinks and he had not. Had he, she wondered, noticed her eagerness to drink? Did he have a problem from which he was recovering? Indeed he did; and he went on to shed his anonymity and tell his story. He also came from a drinking family; like Michelle, he did not have a low bottom, a "fall on his face" end to his drinking. He was a "high bottom" person. With the help of a therapist, he reviewed the many relationships he had burned through already, even in his young adult years. Closely tied with his drinking was a fear of, or inability to form intimate relationships—with men or women.

At his therapist's encouragement, he went to a series of AA meetings. The community that he experienced there, in addition to practicing the twelve steps toward a daily spiritual program, dramatically changed his life. While he still craved alcohol on occasions, AA had brought a peace to his life that he had never experienced before. Michelle was weeping at the struggle in Bob's story, a struggle she secretly shared—and no one but he had noticed, or cared enough to notice. Bob told Michelle that it would help him in his progress toward sobriety, if he could bring her to an AA meeting—just to see if she liked it, whether it would help her. Bob said with earnestness that helping another person become alcohol-free aids an addict in the journey toward sobriety.

Michelle took a big gulp of her drink. She was frightened, she said. She did not know whether she could stop drinking. She knew, however, that Bob was on target. She had a problem with alcohol, and her life was becoming unmanageable. The myth had been penetrated: It will never happen to me. It had.

The Beatitudes and Powerlessness

Michelle was a nominal Catholic—one of the many Catholic young adults who are baptized, but unawakened, never having had a primary conversion experience. Many of the sayings of Jesus in Scripture eluded her understanding. One which she never understood was the Sermon on the Mount in the Gospel of Matthew, or the sermon on the plain as it appears in Luke. How could one be blest, or happy if they were poor, hungry, criticized, etc.? Where is joy or blessedness in "having not"? She gained a little understanding of Jesus' wisdom as she attempted the first step in her AA program, admitting her powerlessness over alcohol.

Admitting powerlessness over anything or anyone was difficult for Michelle. She was the caretaker of a dysfunctional family. At an early age, she had learned the attitude and behaviors of "control." She grew up convinced that she could control people, situations, and things. Through worry, manipulation, and will power she could make things happen, she felt. Her periods of drinking were a bit of "her letting down her guard," and at least for a few moments, experiencing a release from the emotional burden of controlling. But now her great escape "had" her; she was powerless over alcohol and what it was doing to her emotional, spiritual, physical, and interpersonal life. She was in the same downward spiral that her mother had been in for years.

She needed to abstain from alcohol, to let go of that which "had" her. But she was afraid. What would take its place? What would provide the peace, relaxation, serenity—and sometimes the courage that drinking had afforded her? It was in the fear of *not* drinking and wondering what would take the place of alcohol that the insight of the Beatitudes finally hit her. How could you be happy if you were empty, lost, defeated—powerless? Only if you allowed another power in! Yes—that was the paradoxical message of the Beatitudes. Only when one is void of all false security can he or she allow in the true power, the Higher Power.

A Spiritual Program

Michelle began to work on a daily spiritual program. Daily, conscious contact with God, through meditation, prayer, and exercise began to replace her daily drinking ritual. Stripped of false power, she began to taste Divine Power. Raised a Catholic all of her life, she had never known intimacy with God before. An on-again, off-again church-goer, she never had known community, or closeness, as she knew it in her AA meetings.

THE PURPLE RAINBOW

Six months into her recovery, Michelle had a slip. Over the holidays, at a party, she had some champagne. The floodgates were open again. One drink led to another, and another, and another. Blackout! She woke up the next morning not remembering much. Michelle stopped to see me because of the tremendous guilt she felt at having violated her program. She felt like she was starting out from scratch. I tried to reassure her that a reservoir of strength was built up in her because of her abstinence over the months and her spiritual program.

The next day she went to a meeting and was welcomed by the group. She was surprised at their acceptance and has since come to understand that AA is not for the perfect or for those who have arrived. Rather, like all twelve-step programs, it is for the recovering, the broken who are still healing, those in ongoing need of power and healing from God.

Michelle has met many people who violated their programs as she did. She has served as a reminder to them that one failure need not mean disaster or permanent failure, or serve as a reason to prematurely throw in the therapeutic towel. When we last met, Michelle reflected in wonder on how a family curse had become a source of blessing for her. She was indeed a better, more integral person because of her ongoing bouts with alcohol. She wondered at how another wounded person, Bob, had been so crucial to the beginning of her healing. She wondered also at how her failure, her setback has become a source of encouragement for others who had fallen off their program. Michelle's story is a story of new life already begun in woundedness.

Patrick J. Brennan

The Cry for More...The Cry for Help

Father John Walsh is a Maryknoll priest who has spent extensive time evangelizing in Japan and other parts of Asia. He has frequently spoken, upon his return to the United States, of a phenomenon that he noticed in Japan, but not so much in religious education efforts in the United States. Japanese converts to Catholicism, Walsh reports, sincerely struggle with their decision for Christ and the Church. He does not sense the struggle for meaning and faith that the Japanese experience in the consumerism and cultural Catholicism of many Americans. His reflection on struggle and non-struggle has led Walsh to postulate that indeed struggle is a vital part of the evangelization-conversion process.

Walsh sums this up with two thoughts. First, before one will turn to a Higher Power, a person has to experience "a cry for more," a heartfelt need for the transcendent—for more than job, money, busy-ness, and all that can consume us daily. Secondly, and related to the cry for more, is "the cry for help." This second cry is a realization that the fierce individualism and independence of many people today provides only an illusion of happiness. Self-centeredness, narcissism, the pursuit of self or self-actualization, the pursuit of happiness—all are different sides of the illusion. They comprise a deep, dark hole, called isolation and alienation, into which we can fall, when we try to do it all alone, have it all, or leave all our options open. Walsh's cry for help is the realization of one's need for others, bondedness, community.

THE PURPLE RAINBOW

The beginning of Michelle's healing—the healing of so many people with compulsions and addictions, be they alcohol, food, sex, drugs, etc.—was and is the realization of one's poverty, one's powerlessness, and concomitantly one's need for God and others. Before one allows God and others into one's life, a person has to become weak and poor. Often we do not walk into such vulnerability and poverty willingly. We need to be led there by the Spirit operating in human experience and in other people.

CHAPTER ELEVEN

"Protect Us from All Anxiety"

Maybe that prayer, which Catholics voice after the Lord's Prayer, at the beginning of the communion rite of the Eucharist, is a little presumptuous. Whether God should protect us from all anxiety is questionable. There is eu-stress and dis-stress. Eu-stress is good stress, priming and motivating us for excellence in studies, work, athletics, etc. Dis-stress is that which zaps us of life—biologically, emotionally, and spiritually. So some forms of anxiety and stress are helpful, others are death-dealing. It is a life-long process of discernment to sort out one from the other.

Dr. Robert Eliot, author of *Is It Worth Dying For?*, author also of articles, and a lecturer, has referred to the dis-stress type of anxiety as a disease of choice. It is a learned schema of attitudes, values, and ways of behavior. It is living with the volume cranked up to "10" almost all of the time, rather than realizing that God has gifted us with the ability to modulate our emotional response to people, things, and events. Eliot encourages his patients to continually ask in anxiety-producing situations: "Is it worth dying for?"

I have written a whole other book on this topic, *Spirituality for an Anxious Age*, which deals with the psychological and spiritual causes of anxiety and some antidotes to an anxious lifestyle.

This short reflection is meant to re-echo and underscore the core theme of that book: at the root of much of the anxiety, stress, and depression of our age is a spiritual void or emptiness. In many ways we live in a post-Christian, post-atheistic age. There is not a passion or a quest in many for the spiritual. The soul, spirit, and imagination of so many people have been anesthetized. Thus, when many anxiety-producing situations present themselves, many of us have little to fall back on in terms of coping or integrating skills.

Eliot described himself in one interview as a hard-driven, over-achieving man, unconsciously racing through life looking for attention. He continued to race until his first heart attack. Eliot says it was while recovering from the heart attack that he learned: a) don't sweat the small stuff; b) most of it is small stuff; c) anxiety is giving a dollar's worth of energy to something that deserves only a nickel or a dime's worth.

What is becoming even more alarming is that which I have mentioned elsewhere in this book—how we the anxious adult population are passing on this tendency toward anxiety to our children. Now research and literature abound on caring for a nation of anxious, depressed young people, who have few inner resources or coping skills.

Let me clarify that when I speak of anxiety and stress, I am not speaking of the psychotic kind in which one is severely out of touch with reality. I concur with David Sheehan, author of *The Anxiety Disease*, that depression (repressed anger and/or feelings of loss) usually is not far removed from anxiety. Here also I am speaking mainly of the "garden-variety, neurotic type of depression" more than of the bi-polar disease (manic depressive syndrome) or of psychotic manifestations of depression.

The anxiety, stress, and depression that I write and speak of is the learned kind that we pick up from family, life experiences, and our own subjective perception. What has been a break-through experience for me is to see these dysfunctional emotions less from a "disease" standpoint and more from a learning standpoint. If indeed some of us learned to be anxious or depressed, the good news is that we can unlearn some of those early appropriated lessons. Overcoming emotional difficulties is in part the re-education of feelings and also replacing old strategies of responding to life and people with new strategies.

Anne Wilson Schaef has contributed much in her writing to expand our understanding of addiction. The notion of addiction which hitherto we reserved for substances like alcohol and drugs can be just as accurately used to describe a person's relationship to other people, food, sex, organizations, etc. In fact we can become addicted to the illusionary gratification that a high-stress outlook or lifestyle provides. One can be said to be addicted, in a broad sense, if a person uses a particular pattern of activity for coping; it does not work, but the person persists in using the strategy anyway. I can be addicted, then, to values, life commandments, patterns of behavior that rather than lead me to inner peace actually rob me of fullness of life. In his book *Addiction and Grace*, Dr. Gerald May describes the addiction or "attachment" process as a process of: 1) learning, 2) habit formation, 3) struggle, and 4) reinforcement and increased frequency, in search of desired effects.

Cynthia: A Story

Hannah Hurrand, in her book *Hinds' Feet on High Places*, wrote that some people are born with fearful natures. I put a little different spin on that. Some of us were born with some biochemical neurological predispositions to anxiety and/or depression. Early childhood experiences and family environment often maximize these tendencies. We learn, often by age three, to have fearful and/or negative responses to living. As we age, often these learned approaches to living get in the way of happiness, effectiveness at work, or healthy relationships.

Cynthia is in her early twenties, the youngest of five children. The atmosphere in her family was often high-strung and stress-filled. Family values that were stressed as she grew up were productivity, excellence, competition, and high achievement. Being the youngest, she always felt as if she were in a race trying to keep up with stories of the achievements of her older brothers and sisters. Often she felt that she could not, so she would unconsciously opt out. She developed a number of psychosomatic symptoms of a digestive, gastrointestinal nature that from early childhood allowed her to excuse herself or be excused from the front-line of life.

As she turned twenty-one, Cynthia began to date and fell in love with Jack. Even in intimacy, she wanted "to do well," and thus developed a lot of stressful psychosomatic symptoms before each encounter with him. It was a kind of "date fright" that initially brought her to me. Over some weeks I took Cynthia through some steps that I have found helpful—both in managing my own anxiety and fear and in helping others.

1) First of all, in situations of anxiety, stress, or depression, we need to deal with the presenting symptoms. Techniques can be experimented with for reducing the emotional pain in particular situations. In Cynthia's case, I asked her to openly admit to her boyfriend that if she seemed quiet or distant when with him or his family, it was because she was a shy and somewhat anxious person. Openly admitting to the problem immediately robs "the demon" of some of its power. When nervousness made eating at such gatherings difficult for her, I encouraged her to manage the situation by taking only small portions, lowering everyone's expectations, including her own, of how much she should/could eat. Not fleeing, but rather immersing oneself in a situation of disease is

quite important in de-sensitizing oneself to anxiety-producing or depression-producing stimuli. In the immersion, a person learns to re-shape the situations to better fit him or her rather than to allow the situation to take over and destabilize the person. Only when the pain or discomfort of symptoms is dealt with to some degree of success will someone be willing to go more deeply into the process of growth or re-learning.

2) When a person like Cynthia has had some courage restored relative to the "apparent problems," we can proceed to seek out the "fire producing the smoke." I usually ask folks to tell stories of their early family interactions and to recall some of their earliest memories. The early recollections and family constellation analysis are crucial because they have been etched into the memory bank for a reason. Often attached to these memories are the roots of the person's vision of and approach to life. For example, a man with suicidal ideation in the present, recently told me of multiple childhood and family experiences in which he simply quit if situations were getting too difficult for him. Connecting his early stories of quitting to the present, he saw that suicide was his current method of quitting. He began to see that quitting (including suicide) is a mistaken notion about how to handle one's life. Connecting past stories to his present story, the young man gained insight into a pattern of how he responded to life's difficulties: quitting is a fitting solution.

In a similar way, Cynthia's story of her past revealed a pattern in her lifestyle—in this high-strung family, she consistently played the role of the baby, the inadequate one, the one who could not compete or keep up with the rest. Her father appeared as a looming figure who would always come and do for Cynthia, what Cynthia felt, in fear, she could not do. Cynthia gained insight into her panic and anxiety attacks. She looked on herself as an incompetent baby, ill-equipped for the complexities of life —like intimacy with a man. Her anxious symptoms were the "excuses" that she used to get herself off the hook of facing life with some degree of courage.

3) As described earlier in this book, decisions are the hinges of the door called growth. The door cannot open without hinges, and people usually do not change without making decisions. Cynthia's new decisions have to do with changing some of her mistaken notions about life that caused her anxiety attacks and psychosomatic symptoms. Cynthia is deciding that it is good to show vulnerability, to admit weakness, to be imperfect, to open oneself to intimacy.

4) But with Cynthia and others, I talk about specific behavior changes that she must practice relative to herself, work, relationships, and all aspects of life. Ameliorating symptoms, gaining insight into one's flawed convictions, making decisions to change are not enough. Internal change needs to be expressed, ritualized, and fostered through decided upon, strategized behavior change. Specifically, Cynthia and I have had to name some of those life situations—often those that center on intimacy or emotional sharing—that cause her some discomfort. Then, through a paradoxical "will to discomfort," Cynthia is struggling to place herself in those sit-

uations. Her behavior change is changing and will change
the emotional tonality of her life.

The Prayer Dimension in Emotional Healing

But where does Cynthia or anyone get the motivation,
the courage, to take the risk and to deliberately intend
and attend to inner and outer growth? Cynthia and I had
a conversation about that one day. I led with this question: "Cynthia, do you pray?" Cynthia is a graduate of
eight years of parochial school on the elementary level
and four years on the high school level. She currently is
enrolled in a Catholic university. "Pray?" she asked with
curiosity. "Why would I pray? Isn't that a sign of need-
ing a crutch?"

I stayed with the theme. "What's so bad about need-
ing a crutch? What if faith and prayer are in part crutches
for our weak humanity? Is that so bad? If you broke your
leg would you be ashamed of the crutch you need to
walk?"

I do not define prayer in my own life simply as a
crutch. But I sensed in Cynthia a resistance to her own
humanity, a fear of being weak and human, a reluctance
to ask for help. Let us return to John Walsh's notion that
faith usually is not even possible until there is a "cry for
more" and a "cry for help."

I shared with Cynthia some of my own story—a life-
long struggle with fear and anxiety. I shared with her my
own need for therapy to correct some of my own mistaken notions about self, others, life, and God. I also in-

cluded in this sharing the time I spent and spend with a spiritual director. The priest-guru knew and saw a side of me that I was not aware of: that I was deeply religious, but not terribly spiritual. Specifically he showed me that I did not live with a lot of trust or a spirit of surrender relative to the God that I claimed to believe in. He suggested that I did not live as if I were convinced that God loved me.

That was about as much theory as the priest gave me. The rest of his impact into my life was proactive. He prayed with me, taught me to pray, commissioned me to pray "like this" in my own private moment. I told Cynthia that it was this new prayerful experience of God, a God who loved me, a God into whose love I could surrender, that energized and fueled all of the other therapeutic things I tried and try to overcome fear.

After our conversation, Cynthia agreed to spend a week and a half experimenting with prayer. When she returned next time, she said: "I have been getting up an hour earlier each day to take a walk. During the walk, I quietly speak to—I guess God—about any thoughts and emotions that I feel welling up within me. Is that prayer?" I assured her that it was. She went on to tell me how this newly discovered dimension in her life made her feel great. I assigned her more homework: try it again!

She did. And she reported another week and a half of deeper peace than she had ever known. She also told the story of how she confronted her mid-life mother who is currently wrestling with symptoms of depression with the question, "Mother, do you pray?" Her mother confessed to having forgotten how to pray. Cynthia said, "Well

THE PURPLE RAINBOW

Pat Brennan reminded me of how to pray; and I have tried it, and it is helping. You should try it, too.''

Never before had I heard such a natural and spontaneous example of what it means to evangelize. Evangelization dies when it is wrapped in the clothes of a program. True evangelization involves one person giving witness to another about how God has transformed his or her life. It is never manipulative. Rather it is invitational, as Jesus always was. In effect, one person says to another: ''I have found God. It has changed me. I welcome you to 'come and see' with me.''

Cynthia evangelized her mother.

I have ministered to many phobic, anxiety-prone people. Person after person has made the discovery that maybe the symptoms of anxiety will never go away, or they will go away for a time but re-surface. The one constant that will never go away and is stronger than fear is the power of God's healing love. Cynthia has broken through to the experience of God's love. It has not completely nor immediately solved all of her problems, but the breakthrough has had a powerfully therapeutic effect.

Transforming Negative Energy into Therapeutic Power

Three items have come to my attention recently that sum up well or say the last word about emotional suffering.

One was a letter from Texas, from a lady who had read one of my previous books. She told a story of twenty years of anxiety attacks and panic feelings which she has

131

had on and off. There has been no clear cut cure or end of suffering for her. But she has learned of the transforming power of prayer in her difficulties. She has also learned that reaching out to other emotionally troubled people is helpful and therapeutic for her. Her experience verifies the AA insight that helping others toward sobriety facilitates the recovery of the one helping. The writer of the letter said that she was committed to placing her struggles and learnings at the service of others that they might recover.

In a similar vein, I received a letter recently from an organization called AIM—Agoraphobics in Motion. AIM is seeking roots in the Chicago area, and its founder was seeking my support. The goal of AIM, and groups like it (COPE, Recovery, etc.) is that recovering people discover their suffering as a source of growth, not only for themselves but also for others.

Thirdly, I was struck recently by articles in the media regarding Kelly McGillis, a popular young actress. Kelly is a young woman who deals and had dealt with much anxiety and depression. Unlike the many examples in this chapter, in which anxiety and depression have been learned, Kelly's emotional problems were and are the result of her being the victim of a group rape. She tells of how she confined the story of the rape to herself and her family, ashamed to tell others of the incident. She felt vaguely guilty, as if she somehow had brought it on herself. She describes her thinking regarding this incident as completely idiosyncratic and irrational.

Out of acute pain, Kelly has come forward to tell her story to both a therapist and the public. In her secrecy, she confesses, she was allowing her terrorists to control her life. She also has begun to invest money and her acting ability in the production of films that help runaways, who often become the victims of sexual abuse.

Notice what this young woman and the two other examples are doing. In the pain of their lives, they are experiencing the birthing of new possibilities. It is like the death of a forest by fire. While the forest still smolders, new green begins to sprout. Without using theological language, the Texas lady, the founder of AIM, and the young actress have already tapped into the power of the paschal mystery. While we are still hanging on our crosses, the Spirit of God has already begun to transform them into empty tombs.

CHAPTER TWELVE

Beyond Resuscitation

We sometimes mistakenly think that the Easter event was about Jesus *returning* to life, that His Resurrection was a kind of *resuscitation* that restored Him to His previous state. Luke's scene with Thomas disabuses us of such a notion. Jesus tells Thomas to put his finger into the wounds that still are part of the glorified Lord. The Risen Jesus was simultaneously crucified and glorified, wounded and risen, afflicted and transformed. So, the Resurrection was a break-through to a new dimension of being. The wounds of Christ were the threshold experience that led to resurrection, glorification.

The paschal mystery, resurrection, and glorification in our lives does not, will not mean the transcending of our vulnerability or woundedness. Like the woman who wrote from Texas, mentioned in the previous chapter, some of us may carry a specific kind of woundedness around with us in a chronic state. Rather than escaping wounds, often our wounds are the occasion of a new

134

kind of growth—not a return to a previous state, but a penetration into a new dimension of life.

Learning to Trust the Pasch

All the examples and stories in this book reflect a common pattern. The pattern is something like this:

—People are trying to go about the business of "normal living."

—Something, someone comes uninvited into the fabric of their lives.

—That entrance into their lives causes a loss of equilibrium or balance; for many, the loss of homeostasis of balance is quite painful and debilitating.

—After trying to escape the situation of woundedness or pain, people somehow learn to accept a situation of "no escape," that they are indeed struggling and suffering.

—Someone or something in the midst of their struggle awakens them to a Higher Power with them in their pain.

—The Higher Power is imagined, or re-imagined, not as the source or cause of malady, but as therapeutic energy and power in the midst of the pain.

135

Patrick J. Brennan

—Gradually, the wounded learn to surrender to this therapeutic, divine power—not in an attempt to manipulate the divine power, but in the conviction that the power is good and will work to the good of the suffering person.

—Usually there follows a discipline of prayer, meditation, or some kind of "practicing the presence of God." The wounded person lives no longer of himself or herself. The divine lives with and within.

—Gradually, sometimes suddenly, there is a moment of recognition that the divine power has taken the woundedness of one's life and is using it and transforming it for new learning and growth.

—Experiencing a taste of spiritual transformation, the wounded person learns to trust the process. This is somehow how it works—from life, through death, to new life. Vulnerability and woundedness become less feared, because the person knows, is convinced, trusts that divine power, co-operated with, in the mystery of things, transforms breakdowns into breakthroughs.

—Thus, the next shipwreck will be less resisted perhaps. The person involved has begun to trust the process of paschal, or passage living.

On Imagination and Mentors

We hear much about the importance of conversion of heart in the spiritual life. But conversion or spiritual

136

transformation is about changing one's imagination. Among some of us there is an initial resistance to speak of spiritual growth in terms of imagination. We often equate the imagination with the imaginary. Nothing could be further from the truth. Within each of us, the imagination functions as the deposit, the home of our dominant images—those values, perceptions, and symbols that motivate, animate, and drive us.

Advertisers know the power of the imagination. Through the use of symbols, they can convince us in seconds that what life is all about is beer, cars, deodorants, perfumes, or other mythical "its" that we "really need" for happiness. I have become convinced that once someone begins to trust in the paschal process, the glorified wounds process, one has begun to experience a real shift on the level of imagination. One's dominant images—the filters or lenses, through which one interprets life—have begun to shift. Often the major shift takes the shape of ceasing to interpret one's life in terms of mythical "its" (like success, money, achievement, individualism) and coming to interpret life through the images of the cross and empty tomb, the wounds, and the glorified body, still wounded, but never to be the same.

This is not a rational process. It is reasonable in the sense that a person going through it can explain it, perhaps intellectually defend it. But at root, the movement of the imagination to new paradigms, new dominant images, is an irrational act. It is, indeed, a leap of the imagination. Evangelization is a re-patterning of the dominant images or paradigms in one's imagination.

What enables or facilitates this leap of the imagi-

Patrick J. Brennan

nation? Frequently, in my own life and in the lives of people I have encountered, it is the presence of a person of faith, who knows about glorified wounds—like my spiritual director—and who models surrendering to new dominant images—the cross, the empty tomb, the Father's unconditional love, new life through struggle and death. My woundedness has become glorification through people who have stood by in the struggle, prayed with me, "faithed" with me, and demonstrated to me that they know, understand, and trust the process. The universality of this mentoring, spiritual friend experience critiques loudly the largely cerebral, classroom approach we currently take in religious education.

Will I Ever Be the Same?

In panic, clients, in their woundedness, in their dying and rising, ask the question, "Will I ever be the same?" In panic, in pasch, I often ask it of myself. It is a natural question, but it is the wrong question. It speaks of a longing to return to safe harbor, to what once was, to the self I used to be. Learning to trust the process means gradually realizing some life experiences will forever change me, transform me. Often we cannot return to the comfort of who we were. We need to co-operate with grace in becoming who we are being called to become in the deepest part of our souls.

God, can I return to who I was at 25, 32, 30? Can I return to who I was before I became ill, fell in love, lost a loved one, experienced emotional collapse, was jilted in love, attempted suicide.

THE PURPLE RAINBOW

God gently whispers "no." "You are becoming a spoken word that needs to be seen and heard. You are on purpose. Even your struggle will fertilize and enrich humanity and creation. In your woundedness, you are beautiful, rising to new life, and becoming glorified. No, there is no going back. But remember, in the unending, uncharted waters of newness you are never alone. As surely as I did with Moses, I will go with you. So . . . trust."

EPILOGUE

The Purple Rainbow

I dedicated this book to my friend and colleague, Dawn Mayer, whom I described as having entered "the greatest suffering." Like the young lady, Lynn, described in the chapter on suicide, Dawn experienced the suicide of a young man whom she was dating. In the aftermath of the tragedy we have discovered that her friend had deep problems with fear and depression that none of us were aware of. The complication in Dawn's situation was that she was a victim of violence—a hostage held by the young man—until he took his life in her presence.

Despite protestations from both family and me, Dawn attended the funeral of her friend turned attacker, days after the trauma. She said she had to bury the friend she knew for two years, not the unraveled man the rest of us were angry about. Two incidents stand out in the unfolding of this tragedy, both centering on Dawn's faith. The first has to do with the internal workings of her imagination during the hours of the trauma. The second has to do with the funeral.

I asked her, in honesty, how she survived the hostage, violence, self-destructive sequence, and then the police and hospital formalities afterward. She responded that through much of that awful day she sang a song in her head. The song? The words are taken from a black spiritual that we sing at our annual Archdiocesan Black Catholic Revival.

"I love you, I love you,
I love you, Lord, today.
Because you cared for me, in such a special way.
And, yes, I praise you,
I lift you up and I magnify your name . . .
That's why my heart is filled with praise."

Notice in this example, the role of imagination in faith, and the role of faith in healing and helping. In the face of death, this young woman's imagination leapt to images of divine love, conviction of being cared for, and offering divine praise.

As she drove with her family to the cemetery, Dawn noticed a rainbow in the sky over the cemetery. The only special detail that she noticed about the rainbow was that it was totally purple. It was not multi-colored as many rainbows are, just purple. She wondered in her heart if God might be leaving some hint, some clue of his reassuring presence, that she would recover, that her friend—now on the other side of death—was secure.

She did not mention the rainbow until some days later, when she told of it to Patti, her friend, an artistic, sensitive girl, who promptly did research on purple rainbows. She found in a resource book that purple rainbows are among the rarest of rainbows, reported in American meteorological records only twice. The purple rainbow requires a unique blending of sun, atmosphere, and moisture. Patti jubilantly called Dawn and reported her findings about the purple rainbow—especially their rare occurrence.

"Do you think," Dawn tearfully, painfully asked, "that that was a sign, a sign that he is OK...a sign I'll be OK?"

"What do you feel?" I asked.

"I do," she responded. I hope so; and I also believe it.

Dawn's most prized Christmas present this year was a portrait of a purple rainbow which Patti painted for her, and which hangs now in a prominant place in her home. The image of the purple rainbow has not washed away the hurt and trauma. Rather as Dawn still stands in the rubble, it helps her imagination leap from wounds to glorified wounds.

Another Rainbow . . . With a Jet
. . . and Eagles' Wings

When I told Dawn's story of the energizing, therapeutic image of the purple rainbow, a woman approached me with a counter-story that had been triggered in her. She had recently lost her mother to cancer; and she, the daughter, was taking the progressive, inevitable loss with much difficulty. Driving from her comatose mother's home one day, she looked through her wind-

THE PURPLE RAINBOW

shield to a multi-colored rainbow just ahead of her in the sky. As she was struck by its beauty, she saw it penetrated, then transcended by a jet airliner. "I don't know why," she said, "but I knew at that moment that mom would die that day. But I felt great peace. The plane and the rainbow remind me of the song 'Eagles' Wings' . . . 'And he shall raise you up on eagles' wings, bear you on the breath of dawn.'" The woman's imagination had jumped; she had had an intrusive intuition—nonrational in nature. Her mother would die soon; but a force and energy of love would carry her to peace and security. She called her sister who was caring for the mother, and told her that their mother would die that day, but that God was carrying her home. The old woman died later that day.

Another woman told me recently of moving her octogenerian father from the family home of forty plus years to a safer environment. Crime in the neighborhood had risen dramatically. She said that the three family cars carrying her father's things to the new house reminded her initially of a funeral procession. A true death was being experienced. The death of a family home, as described in an early chapter. As "the funeral procession" turned a corner, the woman observed one of the last senior citizens in the old neighborhood taking a walk. His daily constitutional, which she had witnessed for years, was different this time. He had a companion, a muzzled German shepherd who now accompanied him wherever he went. The dog could be easily unmuzzled in case his master were under attack. The grieving daughter had a "purple rainbow" jump of the imagination. "This is no longer a neighborhood," she thought. "This is a concentration camp, or a war zone, where you need an attack dog for protection." Quickly her image of a funeral procession was transformed to the image of a parade. The three-car procession was now a parade celebrating a new beginning, a new life for father and the family.

On Revelation

Revelation is that dimension of spirituality and theology that speaks of God showing himself in human history, in the human story. Too many folks have connotations of revelation that speak of a God who showed himself only in the past to our spiritual ancestors. Too many others look on revelation as God manifesting himself and his will through the magisterial pronouncements of the Pope or councils. We need to re-image, re-imagine revelation, not as history or doctrinal pronouncement. Revelation is rather God showing himself, offering a ray of hope, a feeling of comfort, a challenge now in the present. God's revelation is intuited on the level of imagination. The imagination jumps, often from images of despair, or from breakdown to hope and breakthrough, from wounds to glorified wounds. Revelation is all about purple rainbows, rainbows and jets, and funeral processions that become new beginning parades.

On Sealing Off and Entering Into

The purple rainbow, the hope, the breakthrough alluded to in this book, comes only at a price, the price of being willing to enter into the specific void or pain of one's particular life circumstance. Often we try to seal emotional pain off, to sweep it away. On occasion, when the pain is multi-leveled, as Dawn's was and is, perhaps pieces have to be sealed off temporarily, so that we are not overwhelmed. Then, in our own time, we can break the seal and enter in. But key is "entering into the pain," as it has been variously described in this book. Those who "seal off" pain appear to be the more immediately healthy after a trauma or loss, but in the long run have greater and more protracted periods of suffering. Those who enter into the void or pain appear to have messier, falling apart lives. But their long run prognosis is better, for they begin to confront the pain that only time, love, inner resources, and God can heal.

"Sealing off" is nice and tidy.

Only "entering in," however, creates the possibility of glimpsing a purple rainbow.